When
Bad
Things
Happen to
Good
Knitters

REVISED, EXPANDED, AND UPDATED SURVIVAL GUIDE
FOR EVERY KNITTING EMERGENCY

Marion Edmonds & Ahza Moore

The Taunton Press

TO OUR FIRST KNITTING TEACHERS, AUNTY MIMI AND MRS. MAURIC

The Taunton Press, Inc., 63 South Main Street, PO Box 5506, Newtown, CT 06470-5506
e-mail: tp@taunton.com

Executive Editor: Shawna Mullen
Editors: Rebecca Behan, Carolyn Mandarano, Renée Neiger
Copy editor: Betty Christiansen
Indexer: Cathy Goddard
Jacket/Cover design: Alison Wilkes
Interior design: First edition design by 3+ Co.; revised and updated edition design by Rita Sowins / Sowins Design
Layout: Rita Sowins / Sowins Design
Cover illustrator: Peter Horjus
Interior illustrator: Harry Bates
Photographer: Sara Wight
Stylist: Angela Hastings

The following names/manufacturers appearing in *When Bad Things Happen to Good Knitters* are trademarks: LB Collection®, Lion Brand® Yarn, Rowan®.

Stand Yarn Weight System and needle and hook sizing information courtesy of the Craft Yarn Council, www.yarnstandards.com

Library of Congress Cataloging-in-Publication Data

Edmonds, Marion.
  When bad things happen to good knitters : revised, expanded, and updated survival guide for every knitting emergency / Marion Edmonds, Ahza Moore. -- [Revised, updated and expanded edition].
      pages cm
   ISBN 978-1-62113-007-9 (pbk.)
  1. Knitting. I. Moore, Ahza. II. Title.
   TT820.E4415 2014
   746.43'2--dc23

                          2013026927

Printed in the United States of America
10 9 8 7 6 5 4 3 2 1

Acknowledgments

We would like to thank our Executive Editor, Shawna Mullen. Without her perseverance we wouldn't have had the opportunity to revise and update our book. Many thanks to our Editor, Rebecca Behan, for all her help and guidance. We couldn't have asked for a better companion on our journey. Thanks to Editor, Renee Neiger, who kept us on schedule. (Privately we refer to them as the Three Graces.) Special thanks to Carolyn Mandarano, The Senior Manager who worked tirelessly behind the scenes to bring this edition to print.

Additional thanks go to Lion Brand® Yarn and Rowan® Yarn for providing us with the yarn for our patterns.

Thanks to every one of our knitting students, past, present, and future.

And, last but not least, thanks to our husbands, Lester Rapaport and Vincent Moore, for their love and support.

Contents

Bringing You Up to Date

Dear Fellow Knitters,

We are thrilled to have been asked to update and expand *When Bad Things Happen to Good Knitters.* After we finished the first edition, we found that we had more that we wanted to tell you, and the feedback from those of you who bought our book (may your needles never break) told us that there is more you want to learn. We're happy to oblige you, both our new and returning readers. We've updated our book with our latest finds and added two new chapters that explore some of our favorite techniques and present six charming (if we do say so ourselves) patterns.

In Chapter 5: Further Adventures in Knitting, we introduce you to color, lace, and cables. Here you'll discover beneficial techniques (such as knitting backward and knitting with yarn in either hand) that will make knitting intarsia, Fair Isle, and mosaic patterns easier and way more fun. We go on to explain the basics of lace knitting, and to rip away the Veil of Mystery that surrounds cabling. Along with each new technique come our favorite methods and, as always, how to address the new emergencies that you may face.

You'll now be ready for Chapter 6: Apply Yourself, which contains six patterns we've created to explore the specific techniques that you learned in the previous chapter. Not all in one pattern, of course.

In the years since the first edition, our lives have changed along with our knitting. Ahza moved to Albuquerque, New Mexico, and has been teaching and giving workshops there. Marion stayed in New York City, continuing to teach knitters of all levels. Our separation has brought rewards, of course. We've both learned to make video calls over the Internet, discovered the annual Taos Wool Festival, and explored the many new yarn stores in and around Albuquerque. We spend at least a month together in our respective hometowns each year, just knitting together.

Yours in Wool,
Ahza and Marion, 2013

Introduction to the First Edition

Work is over. The dog is walked. The dishes are done. Finally, it's your knitting time.

You settle into your favorite chair and take up your needles. And then you see it: a stitch that has fallen off one needle and is rapidly unraveling. You watch with fascinated horror as it slips down, row after row. What do you do? You don't know how to fix this disaster and, until you do, you can't continue. It's much too late to call a fellow knitter or expect your friendly neighborhood yarn store to be open. Where to look for an answer?

Right here. We have written this book for you. Turn to "Ohmygawd, I've Dropped a Stitch" on p. 68 and your troubles (at least your knitting troubles) will be over. Our first advice, to any level knitter, is not to panic—this is not the end of the world as you know it. Take several deep breaths, read through the possible solutions, choose one that works for you, apply it, and knit on. Perhaps you already know how to pick up dropped stitches—but that doesn't mean you're emergency free. Maybe you're having trouble decoding a pattern or figuring out what's gone wrong with the neckline you just put in. Perhaps you've mislaid your cable needle. This book is written for you, too.

When Bad Things Happen to Good Knitters is for both the beginning and the more advanced knitter. Its purpose is to help you, and it's written in plain English in case you are not yet fluent in the language of knitting. We've made the headings very clear so that you can easily match your emergency with a solution. We also tell you when mistakes can successfully be fudged and when they can't. Most important, we give you full permission *not* to correct an error. Most of us knit for relaxation, and if just the thought of ripping out six 30-in. rows to fix a misplaced cable gives you palpitations, then let it be. After all, do you really care about the opinion of the total stranger who is inspecting your sweater with a magnifying glass? Many of our favorite knitted creations contain problem spots that we've decided not to fix.

The book begins with "Emergency Prevention, or A Stitch in Time," which will help you assemble your Knitter's Tool Kit and choose yarns and needles that will make your knitting pleasurable. There, you'll find suggestions for good knitting habits you can adopt to help keep your crises to the barest minimum. Chapter 2, "The Secret Language of Knitting Patterns," will help you choose the pattern that's right for you and provides guidance on how to read and follow it. We've also included a section on altering patterns for different sizes and different gauge. "Good Knitting Gone Wrong," includes the most common emergencies we've encountered in our years of knitting and teaching and gives you the skills needed to fix them. In the final chapter, "Don't Let Finishing Finish You Off," we guide you through the finishing process, including how to fix a piece that doesn't fit right. We even have a few ideas for what to do if you end up absolutely hating the fiber fruit of your labors.

When Bad Things Happen to Good Knitters is written to help you out of a jam. Because we don't think that you should have to decide in the wee hours of the morning which of several techniques to use, we've tried to give you only one solution. If you discover others that suit you better, use them. What you knit is yours and yours alone. Sometimes it's hard to remember this when several people are giving you advice and telling you the "right" way to do things. Trust us, no way is the right way for everyone, and since it's *your* knitting, you can do what you please.

We believe that knitting is more than a system for manipulating needles and yarn—it is a path to self-knowledge. The things we learn about ourselves as we knit often have interesting applications in our non-knitting life. Observing how you go about your knitting reveals, for example, whether you are result oriented or process oriented. Do you knit things just because you think they are interesting, without an intended recipient in mind, or do you plan a use for each project before you knit it? How much uncertainty is comfortable for you? Can you imagine starting a sweater and ending up with a pillow for the couch, or do you want every stitch exactly where the pattern says it should be? Can you live with your mistakes, or will you be forever haunted by those extra stitches or that lumpy seam? Fortunately, our craft is wonderfully idiosyncratic (did you know that the knit stitch can be formed four different ways?) and remarkably diverse: There is room for all sorts of knitters, from the most exacting to the most carefree.

You and your knitting are in very good hands—ours. We have each been knitting since the age of four and between us we have 119 years of experience. In fact, yarn brought us together. We saw each other knitting in a coffee shop in New York City and introduced ourselves. Soon we were spending more and more time knitting together, sharing our yarn stashes and trade secrets, and we realized

that after long and varied careers, each of us was at a professional loose end (so to speak). That's when we had the idea of starting a business that would allow us to do what we love best, and that's how our company, KnittingTogetherNYC, was born.

Since then, we've taught hundreds of people to knit, and we hope they've all taught hundreds more. Our dream is for everyone on the island of Manhattan and beyond to experience the benefits of knitting—stress reduction, self-knowledge, the pleasure of creating something with your hands, the continuation of an age-old craft, and a short vacation from our everyday lives. Our worst fear is that when practitioners hit a snag, they become so aggravated that they give up on knitting altogether, and that's why we've written this book.

To guarantee that you get all the pleasure and satisfaction knitting can give, and none of the frustration it can inflict, we have provided you with a safety net—*When Bad Things Happen to Good Knitters.* Don't cast on without it!

**Yours in Wool,
Ahza and Marion**

1

Emergency Prevention, or A Stitch in Time

The truth in knitting is that the vast majority of emergencies can be avoided if you develop good knitting habits. When you're not in the midst of a Panic-Stricken Knitting Event, sit down and read this chapter over. The time you invest in doing this will most likely save you a world of grief later on.

Keep a Knitter's Tool Kit

The purpose of a Knitter's Tool Kit is to provide you with all the necessary items (other than needles and yarn) for knitting or finishing a project. Like a regular tool kit, it contains the equipment you're likely to need on a fairly consistent basis plus other less-used tools that can turn out to be real lifesavers when you find you suddenly need them. Trust us—never leave home without it.

Your kit should include:

- **This book.**

- **Needle sizer:** This is a flat sheet of plastic or metal pierced with holes of various sizes that you can use to determine the size of your needles, particularly useful when you can't remember if the number on your needle is U.S., U.K., or metric. The edges are often calibrated in inches and millimeters, so you can also use it as a small ruler or gauge checker.

- **Tape measure:** You should have one that reads in both centimeters and inches. Use it for measuring your gauge swatch, the person the project is intended for, and your knitting.

- **A pair of small scissors:** These should be sharp and pointed.

- **Stitch markers:** These are circles, plain or fancy, that you put around your needle to help keep your place in a row or round. Some open like safety pins so you can attach them anywhere on your knitting and take them off again.

- **Stitch holders:** You'll need large and small ones to hold live (unworked) stitches that will be worked again later. One type of holder looks like a big safety pin. You undo it, slide the stitches on the open end, and close it up again. When you want to use the stitches, slide them back onto your needle. The other kind is essentially a double-pointed knitting needle that snaps into a bizarre-looking rubber band. Its advantage is that you can knit on and off the holder from either end.

- **Safety pins large and small:** Stock up on coilless knitters' pins, if you can find them. These can be used to rescue dropped stitches that you want to deal with later or to hold a few live stitches when a stitch holder would be too bulky. They also make good row markers.

- **Row counter:** Some hang off the needle, so you can place the counter between stitches; others are freestanding, which you must remember to tap when you finish each row; and still others (which we prefer) slip onto your needle and must be turned each time you complete a row.

- **Point protectors:** These keep your stitches from falling off your needles when you lay your knitting down. They are especially useful when you need to convert double-pointed needles into single-pointed ones.

- **Crochet hooks:** Sizes A, F, and J will cover most situations. These are indispensable for pulling up dropped stitches (see p. 71), crocheting edgings, and making fringe.

- **Tapestry needles:** You'll need these to sew seams, repair mistakes, and weave in yarn ends. They should be large enough not to split the yarn and should have blunt tips and large eyes. We prefer the ones with curved points. Buy various sizes as you need them.

Knitting on the Fly

If you are planning to travel on an airplane *within* the United States, check the Transportation Security Administration's (TSA's) website (www.tsa.gov) for the most current information on taking knitting needles and scissors onboard a plane. Currently, knitting needles and scissors (with blades less than 4 in. long) are allowed. You can take a printout of the TSA's "Permitted and Prohibited Items" list with you to the airport, but ultimately what you are allowed to take onboard is determined by the individual gate agent or TSA representative who inspects your carryon bags.

It's not a good idea to argue with the security agents, so be prepared in case you're told you can't take your precious mahogany needles on the plane with you. Bring a container for your needles so they can be checked as baggage or bring along a self-addressed, postage-paid envelope so you can mail them home to yourself.

For foreign travel, check with each carrier you'll be flying to find out its regulations and those of the country to which you are flying. Keep those self-addressed envelopes handy.

If you're wondering which needles have the best chance of making an international flight with you, Denise Needles (www.knitdenise.com) is your answer. They are sold as a set of needle points of various sizes that attach to cords of various lengths. The points are shorter than a pen and made of resin. Denise's owner, Linda Krag, confirms that the needles are airline safe as long as knitting needles are not expressly forbidden.

- **T-pins and plastic head pins:** These are used for blocking and for pinning pieces together before joining.

- **Lengths of waste yarn:** You can use these for a provisional cast on (see p. 29), when you want to take something off the needles to try on, and as a substitute for stitch holders and markers (see p. 58).

Always Make a Gauge Swatch Before You Begin a Project

Gauge, in knitting, is the number of stitches there are in a fixed width and the number of rows in a fixed height of knitted fabric. Every pattern ever written (okay, maybe there are a few exceptions out there somewhere) is based on a particular gauge, which is noted at the beginning of the pattern's directions. The purpose of knitting a gauge swatch is to make

Basic Knitter's Tool Kit

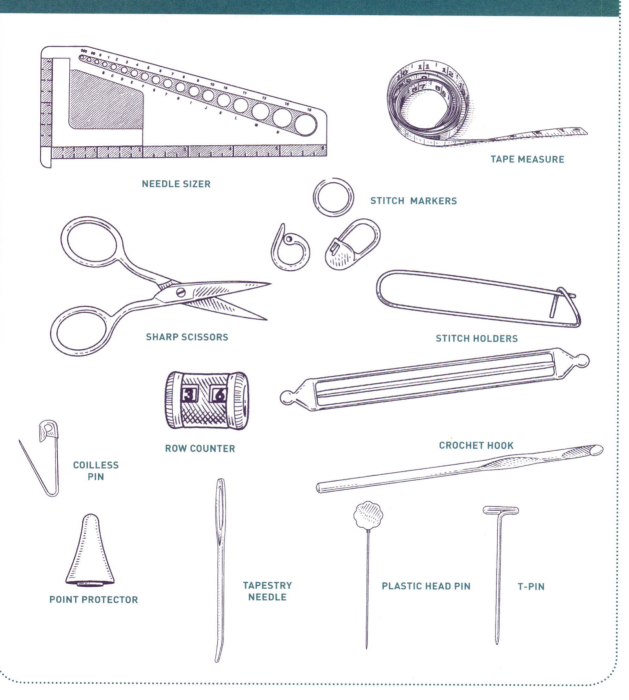

NEEDLE SIZER

TAPE MEASURE

STITCH MARKERS

SHARP SCISSORS

STITCH HOLDERS

ROW COUNTER

CROCHET HOOK

COILLESS PIN

POINT PROTECTOR

TAPESTRY NEEDLE

PLASTIC HEAD PIN

T-PIN

sure that what you knit ends up the same size as the measurements given in the pattern.

Making a gauge swatch is *essential* if you are knitting something that needs to fit, and/or you are not using the specific yarn called for in the pattern. What if you're using exactly the same yarn and exactly the same needles specified in the pattern? Do you still need to knit a swatch? Yes, you do, because you may not knit with the same tension as the pattern writer, and it's better to know that now—not after you suddenly realize your cute, tight summer sweater looks as if it were made to fit someone three sizes bigger than you.

We know knitting a swatch isn't as much fun as actually starting your project. But, believe us, making a swatch is a most excellent example of the old adage "A stitch in time saves nine."

If your pattern includes directions on how to make the gauge swatch, follow them exactly. Otherwise, give our directions a whirl. If you can stand it, buy only one ball of your chosen yarn, take it home, and make your swatch. Return to the store for the rest when you're sure the yarn will work. If you feel you must buy enough yarn for the entire project, *keep the receipt* (this is always a good idea; if you have leftover yarn, you might be able to return it for store credit).

THE NO-FAIL GAUGE SWATCH

Using the needle size suggested in the pattern and the number of stitches to the inch suggested by the gauge, cast on enough stitches to make a swatch 4 in. wide plus 6 sts. Work the first 4 rows in garter stitch. Then change to the appropriate stitch pattern, beginning and ending each row with 3 knit sts (that means front and back), and knit the number of rows that should give you 4 in. of knitting (don't count the garter stitch rows that you began with). Then finish the swatch off with 4 more rows of garter stitch and bind off loosely.

For example, if the gauge in the pattern calls for 20 sts to equal 4 in. across and 24 rows to be 4 in. high, you would cast on 26 sts (20 sts plus 6 sts); knit 4 rows in garter stitch; and then work 24 rows in the pattern, starting and ending with 3 knit sts on every row. End the swatch with 4 more rows of garter stitch and a loose bind off.

Now for the moment of truth. If you can stand to wait, wash and block the swatch before measuring. This step lets you find out *before* you knit and launder your finished garment that

A Cautionary Tale

One fall, Marion raced to knit five sweaters and vests of various designs for her five best friends for Christmas. All five sweaters were beautiful. But, because she had not done gauge swatches, not even one of the sweaters fit even one of her five best friends. She spent four miserable months ripping, making gauge swatches, and reknitting. She promised herself she would always make gauge swatches from then on—and, mostly, she has.

Adjusting the gauge horizontally (stitches to the inch)

If you have *fewer* stitches per inch than the gauge calls for (say you're getting 4 sts per inch instead of 5 sts), your garment will be too large if you don't adjust your gauge. Knit another swatch using the next smaller size needles to get more stitches to the inch. If that still doesn't get you where you need to be, keep changing to the next smaller size needles until the horizontal gauge is correct or the yarn is too tight to knit, in which case, you have to face facts and choose another yarn for this project.

If you need to experiment with several different needle sizes in your search for gauge, you don't need to start your swatch over again each time; just separate the different needles' swatches by knitting 2 rows of garter stitch between them.

If you have *more* stitches per inch than the gauge calls for (say, 6 sts to the inch instead of 5 sts), your garment will be too small. Swatch again using the next larger size needles to get fewer stitches to the inch. Use larger and larger needles until the horizontal gauge is correct or the resulting fabric is too loose for its intended purpose. If you still want to use this yarn, try combining it with another strand of itself or another yarn. But, again, at some point you may need to accept that this yarn just isn't going to work with this particular project.

Adjusting the gauge vertically (rows to the inch)

The row gauge doesn't matter as much as the horizontal gauge because usually the pattern gives vertical measurements in inches or centimeters. Just follow the pattern instructions, knowing that you may knit fewer or more rows than the pattern calls for. Unless you are cabling, knitting a multirow pattern, or doing color work, you'll be just fine.

If your row gauge doesn't match the pattern and the pattern uses the number of rows as

washing it is going to add 2 in. to the length or that the red yarn you've chosen for a stripe turns the white yarn it's paired with a pale pink when the yarns hit water. Once dry (or right away, if you can't wait), lay the finished swatch on a flat surface. Measure 2 in. by 2 in. in the middle of the swatch, count the number of stitches and rows, and check if they match the gauge given in the pattern—for our example, 5 sts per inch across and 6 rows per inch, or some multiple thereof, in height. Measure in more than one spot just to be sure.

Please be honest with yourself when you measure your swatch, especially if this is a garment that needs to fit. Even a small difference in gauge can have serious consequences.

If your gauge swatch doesn't match the pattern gauge, don't worry. After all, the gauge is an expression of that particular designer's knitting eccentricities and is not written in stone. We have solutions for getting the gauge you want without abandoning the yarn you want—well, most of the time.

the vertical measurement, here's what to do. Turn the number of pattern rows into inches (using the pattern gauge), and then multiply the inches by *your* rows per inch. The result will be the number of rows you need to knit. Replace the number of rows given in the pattern with the number based on your swatch, and you're all set.

For example, suppose you get 7 rows to the inch and the pattern calls for 6, but you are on gauge horizontally. You'll do fine until the pattern tells you to work 96 rows. If you follow the instruction as written, the length of what you've knit will be too short. So, how many rows should you knit?

STEP 1

- Divide the number of rows in the pattern by the pattern gauge's rows to the inch. The result is the height of all the rows in inches.

96 rows ÷ 6 rows to the inch = 16 in.

STEP 2

- Multiply the result (the height) by your vertical gauge to get the number of rows you need to knit.

16 in. x 7 rows to the inch = 112 rows

- Makes sense, doesn't it? Because your rows are shorter than what the pattern gauge calls for, you have to knit more of them.

WHEN YOU JUST CAN'T GET TO GAUGE

If you can't achieve gauge or get there with acceptable results by doing the needle fandango, there is one more alternative if you just can't bear giving up your yarn. That's to adjust the pattern. For more on that, see "Biting the Bullet, or How to Adjust a Pattern for Size" on p. 36.

THE LESSONS OF GAUGE

The humble gauge swatch reveals other things, too. It shows you how the yarn looks when knit up so you can decide if you really like it. More

---

⊛ The Perils of Not Paying Attention to Gauge

Let's say the pattern gauge is 4 sts to the inch (16 sts to 4 in.), but your gauge swatch measures 3 sts to the inch (12 sts over 4 in.). Fecklessly, you cast on the 78 sts for the back of the sweater anyway; after all, how big a deal could 1 st per inch be? You'll soon find out that instead of having a 19½-in.-wide sweater back, you have knitted a 26-in.-wide back! We hope that you have a friend with 52-in. hips to whom you can give this sweater.

Getting to Gauge

Here's an example of our No-Fail Gauge Swatch as we try to get to gauge, starting with size 4 needles and ending up with size 6. Each portion of the swatch is separated by 2 rows of garter stitch, and we kept track of the needle size by purling the number into each portion of the swatch.

- Begin and end the swatch with 4 rows of garter st.

- Begin and end each row with 3 knit sts.

- Purl the needle size into each portion of the swatch for permanent reference.

- Separate the different needle size portions of the swatch with 2 rows of garter st.

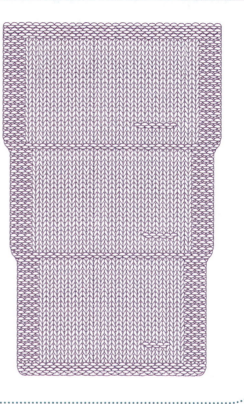

important, it's a test drive of both the yarn and the pattern, allowing you the opportunity to see if you enjoy working with the yarn you've chosen and whether executing the stitch pattern will drive you crazy. Be honest with yourself—if you knit to relax and the yarn or the pattern is giving you palpitations, chances are you'll never finish the project. So save yourself the aggravation, and ditch the yarn and/or save the pattern for another day when perhaps you'll find its complexity engaging.

IF YOU ARE GENETICALLY INCAPABLE OF KNITTING A GAUGE SWATCH

If you *refuse* to make a gauge swatch, we are not going to materialize at your shoulder and slap your hand. But we do have some suggestions for minimizing the chances of finding yourself in a gauge-induced emergency situation:

- Make projects for which gauge is not important—scarves, shawls, and afghans, for example.

- Choose projects for which the exact size of the finished garment doesn't matter. You can present baby sweaters even if they are too large (babies get bigger, after all); if it's too small, save the garment for another, smaller baby. Pillow covers, handbags, and stuffed animals are other good choices.

- Start knitting without making a gauge swatch. Measure the gauge after you are several inches into the garment; and if it's not right, rip everything out and start over with different size needles. Then hope the second or third time will be the charm.

Know What You're Knitting With: Yarn 101

If you are using the exact yarn that is called for in your pattern, you don't need to read this section for your *current* project. But it's a very good idea to give some thought to the yarn you choose.

The extent of a fiber's flexibility is determined by what it's made of. The yarns that come from animals have the most give. Silk, also considered an animal yarn although it comes from an insect, is less flexible. Fibers that come from plants—such as cotton, linen, hemp, and bamboo—often don't change that much when you block them and are more difficult to knit because they aren't flexible. This category also includes synthetic fibers that are derived from natural sources, such as rayon (made from wood chips) and ramie (made from grass).

Yarns come in many sizes (thicknesses), from just a little thicker than sewing cotton to as big around as your thumb. A yarn can be composed of a single strand or many, and it can be tightly twisted or so loosely twisted that the yarn is thick and fluffy in some places and thin in others. Yarns can be one color or many colors. Several colors may be twisted together in one strand or the colors may change within the skein itself, in short or long lengths and in a definite pattern or at random.

Consider, then, the novelty yarns. Infinite in their variety, these yarns can be fuzzy, lumpy, metallic, furry (sometimes made of real fur), or have pieces of different fibers twisted around them or hanging off at intervals. Some are spun around small objects, some look like ribbon, and some look like ladders. Each of these variables can be combined with one another, yielding a seemingly endless choice of yarns that would take a lifetime to explore.

Have we completely overwhelmed you? Would you like some guidance? The following suggestions will help you choose the right yarn for almost any project.

MATCH THE YARN TO YOUR SKILL LEVEL

Beginners do well with yarns that are smooth, flexible, and cling to the needles. Tightly twisted wool or wool-like yarns are perfect.

Also, a yarn that is thick and thin at intervals will conceal a multitude of mistakes in tension. Cotton and linen are also good choices but are less elastic than wool and therefore less forgiving of mistakes. In the beginning, avoid dark colors or a yarn that's the same color as your needles because this makes it hard to see your stitches.

As you become more experienced, you may want to experiment with yarns that are more difficult to knit with—silk or rayon (slippery), mohair or angora (so many hairs that it is nearly impossible to undo the stitches if you make a mistake and need to go back and correct it), and cashmere (which is so expensive that you really need to know what you're doing), just to name a few. After you are comfortable with all these, you are ready to work with novelty yarns. Some are easy to knit with because they mimic traditional yarns, but others present their own challenges.

It's very hard to see individual stitches on the needle if you are using crinkly, furry, or fuzzy yarns (this is true of any kind of yarn that has strands coming off a central core). The remedy is to use lots of stitch markers. Place a marker between each stitch at first, if necessary. Also, knit with needles whose color contrasts with the color of the yarn. Take heart, eventually your needle will learn how to find the stitch on its own.

Metallic yarns, especially dark ones, often share the "I can't find my stitches" syndrome with the "this yarn is devilishly slippery" syndrome. In addition to stitch markers, use wood or, even better, bamboo needles for traction. Knitting metallic yarn on metal needles will drive you crazy.

Yarns made of ribbon, raffia, or chenille knit up best using needles that have long, rather blunt points. Also, if you're compulsive (like Marion), your work will go slowly as you carefully untwist the yarn so each stitch lies flat. If you're not as compulsive (like Ahza), knit fast and the resulting fabric will have a wonderful devil-may-care quality about it.

MATCH THE YARN TO YOUR PROJECT

A good rule of thumb for matching your yarn to your project: simple stitches, fancy yarn; fancy stitches, simple yarn. You don't want to spend untold hours making a cabled sweater out of mohair, which, in its hairiness, will entirely obscure the beauty of your cables. For the same reason, you don't want to use a multicolored, textured yarn for seed stitch. No one will ever be able to tell the knit from the purl stitches.

MATCH THE YARN TO THE RECIPIENT OF THE PROJECT

When knitting a gift, take into account the recipient's possible allergies and preferences. Children are usually very definite in their tastes and will let you know if they don't like

Save Those Swatches!

If you get in the habit of knitting all your swatches as squares described on p. 10, you can sew them together when you have knit enough to become an interesting lap robe or afghan—and a history of the things you've made (or at least started).

STANDARD YARN WEIGHTS

ACTUAL YARN	NUMBERED BALL	DESCRIPTION	Sts/4 in.	NEEDLE SIZE
Lace	**0** LACE	Fingering 10-count crochet thread	33–40**	1.5–2.25 mm (U.S. 000–1)
Super fine	**1** SUPER FINE	Sock, baby, fingering	27–32	2.25–3.25 mm (U.S. 1–3)
Fine	**2** FINE	Sport, baby	23–26	3.25–3.75 mm (U.S. 3–5)
Light	**3** LIGHT	DK, light worsted	21–24	3.75–4.5 mm (U.S. 5–7)
Medium	**4** MEDIUM	Worsted, afghan, Aran	16–20	4.5–5.5 mm (U.S. 7–9)
Bulky	**5** BULKY	Chunky, craft, rug	12–15	5.5–8.0 mm (U.S. 9–11)
Super Bulky	**6** SUPER BULKY	Bulky, roving	6–11	8 mm and larger (U.S. 11 and larger)

The gauges and needle sizes in this chart reflect the guidelines of the Craft Yarn Council of America (CYCA). For more information, visit their website: www.yarnstandards.com.

**Lace weight yarns are usually knitted on larger needles to create lacy, openwork patterns. This makes a recommended gauge range difficult to determine. Always follow the gauge stated in your pattern.

something. Adults are more polite, but it's not nice to take advantage. As well, if you're knitting for a child, you may want to take into consideration the durability of the yarn and how it needs to be laundered. An everyday kid's sweater that needs to be dry-cleaned or requires special washing isn't likely to see a lot of use.

USE YOUR COMMON SENSE

You absolutely adore the one shade of orange that comes only in baby weight yarn, ignoring the fact that you'll need to work it on size 2 needles (U.S.). Do you really think you'll like the shade as much after you've spent a good part of your life knitting it into a king-size afghan for your mother-in-law? (May she live so long and be healthy.)

Making Many into One (Successfully)

When you knit with several different yarns at once, put each ball in its own plastic storage bag, cut a small piece off one of the corners, feed the yarn out of this hole, and reseal the other end of the bag.

When combining yarns, wind each yarn separately. If you wind the yarns together into one large ball, you can bet your favorite cashmere yarn that they will come off the ball unevenly. The only solution, then, is to unwind the combined yarn from the big ball and rewind each yarn into its own ball. This is a fate that we would wish on no one. Also, knit slowly at first, making sure that you pick up all the strands with each stitch.

READ THE LABEL BEFORE YOU BUY

The most important thing of all is to read the label—and remember to keep at least one for future reference. We're firm believers in "If you love a yarn, buy it," but you also need to know if it's suitable for the project you have in mind, and the label is a good place to start because it's chock-full of important information.

The color number or name and dye lot

It's obvious to all of us that yarn comes in different colors; what's not so obvious is the fact that the dye lot is just as important as the specific color name or number. Most yarns are dyed in lots of many skeins, and the same color can vary from one dye lot to the next. There's usually a dye lot number near the color name or number on the yarn label. Make sure you buy all your yarn of the same color from the same dye lot; *double-check before you leave the store.* If you don't do this, you may find yourself inadvertently knitting a two-tone garment. Fortunately, if you find yourself in this unhappy situation, we have a solution (see p. 65).

Fiber content

Some people are allergic to wool or other fibers.

Washing instructions

See p. 101 for details.

Suggested needle size for achieving suggested gauge

If you're not using the yarn called for in a particular pattern, compare the needle size and gauge information given in the pattern to the one on the yarn label. If the two are somewhat similar, go ahead and make your first "No-Fail Gauge Swatch" (see p. 10). If they are very different, you've probably chosen the wrong weight yarn. If you're an advanced knitter, you can rewrite the most complicated pattern without breaking a sweat (see p. 36). If you're an intermediate knitter, look for another yarn— this is our personal choice, and we have more than 125 years of knitting experience between us!

Knit in Haste, Repent at Leisure

Early in her knitting career, Ahza found a pattern for a shirtwaist sweater she loved so much she just *had* to start it right away. It was a pullover with a lovely collar and some rapid decreases on the sides to pull it in at the waist. She found some yarn in her stash with enough yardage and couldn't wait to get started. So what if the yarn was a quite a bit heavier than the pattern suggested—she figured she could use smaller needles to get to gauge. Well, she *almost* got to gauge.

She knew as she worked on the sweater that some things weren't quite right, like the puffed sleeves that would have been lovely and soft in a light-weight yarn—but were stiff and thick in Ahza's yarn. To avoid a scratchy neckline, she used a ball of her best cashmere and knit the collar out of it.

After the sweater was finished, she wore it a few times. It fit all right, but it was way too hot to wear indoors and the wrong style to wear outdoors. Now it rests at the bottom of a drawer, a powerful reminder to ignore the Lessons of Gauge at your peril, as well as to Match Your Yarn to Your Project.

Size (or thickness) of the yarn

There is a movement in the United States to standardize the size information on the yarn label, so if you have chosen a yarn made or packaged in the United States, there may be a picture on your label of a small ball of yarn with a number on it from 0 to 6. The smaller the number, the finer the yarn.

If this symbol isn't on the label, you may find a key word like *lace weight* or *worsted.* Or you can determine the size by matching the suggested needle size and gauge to the chart "Standard Yarn Weights" (on p. 16).

Length of yarn in the skein or ball

This number is useful if you are not using the yarn specified in the pattern and want to know how much yarn to buy.

How much the ball or skein weighs

This bit of information isn't too important, but the relationship between the weight of the ball and its yardage will give you a clue to the size of the yarn if there is no other information. A skein of 100 m that weighs 100 g contains thicker yarn than a skein of the same weight that has a length of 200 m.

Buy the Right Amount of Yarn

Even if you're using the yarn recommended in a particular pattern, buy an extra ball. Usually, you can return any unused balls to the yarn store if you keep the receipt and take the yarn back within a certain period of time (check with your store about its return policy when you

What Label?

It's inevitable that at some point you're going to find yourself labelless and in need of information about the yarn you're using to knit up a project. Don't despair. You can still tease out at least some of the information you need to know about the mystery yarn.

The fiber content

This is important so you can avoid any possible allergic reactions and so you'll know how to wash and block the finished garment (see pp. 99–103). Novelty yarns are almost always synthetic. Otherwise, eyeball the yarn and take a guess. Chew on it. (Man-made yarns feel different. Practice on some of the labeled yarn in your stash.)

If you need to know whether the yarn is 100 percent wool, cut off a 2-in. piece and burn it. If it stinks in an animal sort of way and the ash curls up and breaks apart, it's almost certainly made of natural fiber and most likely wool. If it stinks in an acrid way and the fiber shrivels into ashes without curling up first, it's synthetic.

The size or thickness of the yarn

Compare your yarn to a yarn that has a label (in a yarn shop or one from your stash).

The size needle to try first

Start either by using the needle size suggested by your pattern or the needle size suggested by the thickness of your yarn (see p. 16)

The length of yarn in the ball or skein

Position two objects so the distance around them is 1 yd. Chair backs are good for this. Tie one end of the yarn to one object and wind the yarn around the two objects. When you run out of yarn, count the number of threads on one side of the resulting circle of yarn. That's the number of yards in the ball or skein.

buy the yarn). If you can't return it, simply add the extra yarn to your stash. The exception to the extra ball rule is when you're buying for a pattern that calls for small amounts of many different colors, such as in an argyle pattern. One ball of yarn in each color is likely to be enough. Use your best judgment.

IF YOU'RE USING A DIFFERENT YARN FROM THE ONE USED IN THE PATTERN

Look at the pattern instructions to find out the length of yarn in each of the balls of the recommended yarn. Unfortunately, the pattern doesn't always tell you. If that's the case, ask your local yarn shop or do an Internet search on the yarn until you find a website that gives the yardage. You can also call the yarn company directly.

Once you've got the yardage per ball or skein, figure out the total yardage needed by multiplying the number of balls by the yardage in each ball. Then divide the total by the yardage per ball of yarn you've selected. The result will be the number of balls you need to buy—don't forget to buy that extra ball, of course.

You Lost the Rest of Your Yarn

Cynthia came to us with a big problem. She had been knitting an adorable hat for her friend's child and laid it aside. Now her friend was asking for it. She dug the hat out of her closet only to find that she'd lost the rest of the yarn! She had used a special yarn that had many colors and lots of loops and nubs. And, oh yes, she lost the yarn label, too. Our first suggestion, looking on the Internet for another skein, turned up nothing. Then she admitted that she'd lost the pattern as well.

The hat was almost finished, but not quite. She had about an inch more of decreases to knit before tying it off and weaving in the tail. Our next idea was to finish with a complementary yarn. But the original yarn was so jolly and unique that every other yarn we tried looked very wrong. And that wouldn't solve the lost pattern problem, anyway. So what to do?

Finally, we realized that with some creative thinking, this hat could be ended as it was, with just a couple of decrease rounds to close it up. It would still fit and have a nice shape. So we showed Cynthia that she could frog (unknit) a couple of rounds until she had about 2 yd. of yarn. Then she knit again, decreasing rapidly until she had just a few stitches left. She finished by threading the yarn through the remaining stitches, and tying it off. The child and mother both love the hat!

We encourage thinking creatively. The solution is often hiding in plain sight.

For example, say the pattern calls for 10 balls of Astral Deluxe Yarn. Each ball of that yarn contains 85 yd.

10 (number of balls) x 85 yd. (length of 1 ball) = 850 yd. (total yardage)

Now let's say you want to use Earth's Best Handspun, which has only 50 yd. in each ball. Divide the total yardage (850 yd.) by the yardage in 1 ball of your chosen yarn (50 yd.); the result is 17 balls. (Buy 1 extra, of course.)

850 yd. ÷ 50 yd. = 17 balls (buy 18)

If you're making up your own pattern, find a published pattern that looks like what you are going to create and that uses a yarn of a weight similar to the one you want to use. Figure out the total yardage needed for the published pattern and then how many balls of your chosen yarn you need, as just outlined for the Earth's Best yarn. For this type of project, however, you'd better buy two extra balls.

If you're mathematically challenged or just don't want to work through the equations, then we say, wing it—and we applaud you!

If it turns out you've bought too much yarn, make a matching scarf. If you've not bought enough, you're going to have to improvise, but you'll certainly never see *your* sweater on someone else's back.

Find the Right Needles

Knitting needles come in different combinations of sizes, types, lengths, and materials. With all these choices, there's no excuse for not knitting with needles that please you.

SIZE

Needle size refers to the needle's diameter. Some needles are as thin as wires, whereas others are as thick as your wrist. Many needles

Breaking Up with a Yarn

If you don't like working with the yarn, return it or give it to someone who will love it as much as you do not. There are too many kinds of yarn to choose from to knit with yarn that you don't like. By giving it away, you will give new life to the yarn and make its new owner very happy.

have their sizes etched or printed on them. When you look at the needle packaging, don't confuse this number with the length of the needle. Just to amuse knitters, the numbering systems of needle sizes vary from country to country. And to add insult to injury, needles with the same numbers but made by different manufacturers may be slightly different diameters. In the metric system, needles are measured by millimeters, so the lower the number, the thinner the needle. The U.S. system is comparable—smaller numbers mean thinner needles. In the U.K. and Canada (although these countries are converting to the metric system), needle sizing is just the opposite: The smaller the number, the thicker the needle.

Such complications explain why the needle sizer is a must in your "Basic Knitter's Tool Kit" (see p. 9 for a picture). To use the sizer, pass the tip of your needle through a hole that looks like it matches the needle's diameter. If the shank (the thickest part of the needle) fills the hole, try your needle in the next smaller hole. If it fits easily through that hole, keep going down in size until the needle will no longer pass through it. The size of your needle is the number of the smallest hole through which the shank will pass.

TYPES OF NEEDLES AND THEIR USES

As well as coming in many different sizes and lengths, needles also come in different shapes. Square needles are a relatively new development. By square we mean that the shafts of the needles are square—not that the needles are behind the times. These shapely needles are popular enough to be made in assorted materials, types, and lengths.

Single-pointed needles

These needles are pointed on one end and have something on the other end to keep stitches from falling off the back of the needle. They come in a variety of lengths (6 in. to 16 in.) and sizes (1 to 50 U.S.) and are used to work back and forth to make a flat piece of knitting.

Double-pointed needles

These needles have points on both ends, come in various lengths (4 in. to 16 in.) and sizes (0000000 to 15 U.S.), and are used for knitting around and around to make a tube (such as for a single finger of a glove or for the body of a sweater). They come in sets of four or five. They can be turned into single-pointed needles by putting a point protector at one end or sticking one end into a small piece of cork.

Circular needles

These needles look like two single-pointed needles joined by a flexible, smooth cord (usually made of plastic). The cords come in a variety of lengths (4 in. to 72 in.) and the needles come in sizes 000 to 36 U.S. They are used instead of double-pointed needles for

knitting in the round; the longer ones are especially useful for knitting the borders around afghans or scarves made widthwise. Circular needles can also be used instead of two single-pointed needles to knit back and forth. This has many advantages, the most important of which is that you'll never lose your empty needle. Circular needles are also

NEEDLE CONVERSION CHART

U.S.	Metric (mm)	U.K./Canadian
0	2	14
1	2.25	13
2	2.75	12
	3	11
3	3.25	10
4	3.5	
5	3.75	9
6	4	8
7	4.5	7
8	5	6
9	5.5	5
10	6	4
10.5	6.5	3
	7	2
	7.5	1
11	8	0
13	9	00
15	10	000
17	12	
19	16	
35	19	
50	25	

NEEDLE CHOICES

MATERIAL	PROS	CONS
Wood or bamboo	Very good for beginners, as these needles tend to grip the yarn Warm to the touch	May break in smaller sizes More advanced knitters may find them too slow (again, because they grip the yarn) Larger sizes in wood can be heavy
Metal	Great for knitters who want to knit fast, as the metal surface creates very little friction Cool to the touch The better steel needles will last a lifetime Rarely break or bend, which is very useful in small sizes	Some knitters find them inflexible Too slippery for some When coated with plastic, they are warmer and less slippery We think aluminum needles are the needles from hell because they are too light in weight. But we are nothing if not opinionated
Plastic * These vary the most in quality because there is such variation, our advice is to try before you buy, if you can.	Warm to the touch Some allow the yarn to slide easily	Some catch the yarn Some are hollow and very light but in large sizes they are often quite heavy; we find large hollow needles disconcerting to work with because their weight doesn't match the yarn weight Some have blunt points Some have points that wear down as you knit on them

Don't Lose Your Stitches

If you're knitting in the round, the length of the circular needle needs to be less than the circumference of what you are knitting. However, if the needle is a bit short for the number of stitches you're carrying, be sure to tie or bind the ends of the needles together with a ribbon or rubber band before you put your knitting down. This prevents the stitches from gleefully creeping off the needles when you're not around.

especially useful for knitting in confined places like the subways or on a bus or plane. You can't poke your neighbor with the end of a circular needle because you're knitting with it. They are also a good choice for large projects because many more stitches can fit on the connecting cord than on a straight needle, and the weight is always equally distributed between your hands.

NEEDLE MATERIALS

Needles can be made of a variety of different materials, but in "Needle Choices" on p. 23, we've limited ourselves to evaluating the pros and cons of the most common ones. Ultimately, you should choose the needle that feels best in your hands and fits the type of project you are making. No matter what anyone tells you (including us), there are no right or wrong needles, just the ones you like to knit with.

The exotics

"Exotic" needles are made from ebony, rosewood, ivory (antique), bone, and horn, and even materials we haven't seen yet. Some of these have been carved by hand. By the time you're ready to buy needles as expensive as these, you'll know exactly which ones you like.

Cast On So You Won't Have to Rip Out

There are many different ways to cast on stitches. We've discovered over 40 and we're still finding more. Luckily, you don't need to know that many. And if you're happy with the cast on you're using now, you won't need to read this section until you find yourself in a special situation (believe us, you'll know).

The most important thing about casting on is getting the correct tension. Why? Imagine your beautiful sweater, lovingly knit, carefully pieced together and finished. And imagine not being able to get the bottom row down over your hips. There are a select few who cast on too loosely, but the pressures of living in this modern world have gotten to most of us—and knitters manifest this when they knit (and cast on) too tightly. Because the cast on is done at the beginning of every piece of knitting, it's a *long* way back to rip if it's too tight. However, you will find a solution on p. 97, if you find your cast on is too tight.

If you tend to cast on too tightly, try saying (to yourself, of course), "Loosely, goosey" as you cast on each stitch. Marion does. Or if this embarrasses you (nothing embarrasses Marion), cast on using a larger size needle than you'll be knitting with. Or cast on over two needles held together. These methods always work if you use a large enough needle or needles, but use your judgment. You don't want your cast-on row to end up too loose.

If, after knitting a few rows, you see that the tension of your cast-on row doesn't fit what you're knitting, the best solution is to go back and cast on again. The problem does not magically heal itself, and the cures for cast-on emergencies are all worse than ripping out several rows of knitting.

THE LONG-TAIL CAST ON

If you're not satisfied with your method of casting on, you might want to try the one we use the most, the long-tail cast on. It is quite flexible without being formless and is good for beginning anything from a scarf to a sweater. It's much more difficult to explain than to do, so stay with us and follow the illustrations on p. 26.

1. Start by making a slip knot, leaving a tail that is at least four times the length of the desired finished edge. For example, if the pattern calls for a sweater back that is 18 in. wide, the tail should be at least 72 in. (4 × 18) long. Always be generous. If you're making a sweater with side seams, you can use any extra yarn to sew up the seams. Place the slip knot on the right-hand needle and hold the needle between the thumb and first finger of your right hand.

2. Place the thumb and first finger of your left hand together and put them between the two strands hanging down from the right-hand needle. Separate the thumb and forefinger of your left hand to form a V, so the strand coming from the ball falls around the forefinger, and the yarn that has a tail around the thumb, and grasp the strands lightly with the remaining fingers of your left hand, as shown in Figure 1 on p. 26.

The Importance of Casting On Loosely

When she was 15, Marion knit a pair of argyle socks for her father. They were truly a labor of love because the 7 in. of argyle pattern between the ribbing and the heel, which required 12 bobbins all clacking and tangling together, nearly drove her to distraction. With no regard for her own mental health, she even knit the second sock. Her father was very pleased and touched by her gift and tried them on immediately. "They're absolutely beautiful," he said. "The only thing is, they're too tight at the top. Would you loosen them up, please?"

If Marion had cast on more loosely or been able to buy this book, she wouldn't have had to knit both socks one more time.

The Long-Tail Cast On

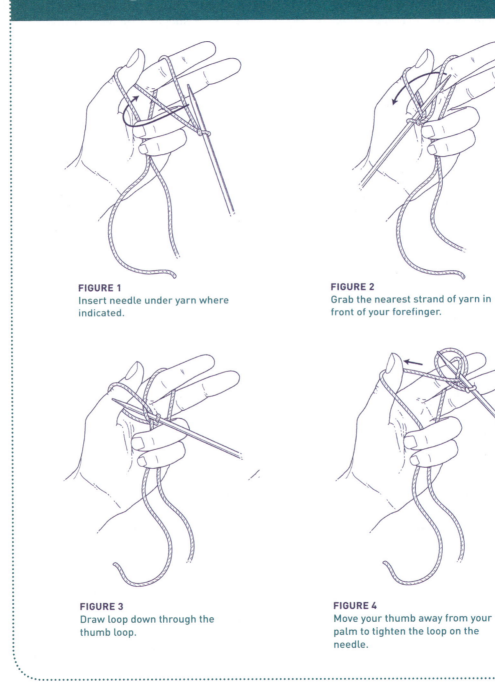

FIGURE 1
Insert needle under yarn where
indicated.

FIGURE 2
Grab the nearest strand of yarn in
front of your forefinger.

FIGURE 3
Draw loop down through the
thumb loop.

FIGURE 4
Move your thumb away from your
palm to tighten the loop on the
needle.

3. Pull the needle toward you and insert the point under the yarn in front of your left thumb, as shown in Figure 1.

4. Releasing more yarn, with your needle, grab the nearest strand of yarn in front of your forefinger and pull it, making a loop on the needle (Figure 2). Draw this loop down through the thumb loop, as shown in Figure 3.

5. Release the yarn wrapped around your left thumb, place your thumb under the front strand you have grasped against your palm, push the yarn toward you (make your original V), and gently widen the thumb and fore finger, still holding the strands of yarn. This widening will tighten the loop on the needle (Figure 4). You should now have 2 sts (the slip knot and the cast-on stitch) on the right-hand needle that are snug *but not tight.* If you have 3 sts or 1 st, please try again.

6. Now take it from Step 3 ad infinitum (or until you have the number of stitches you need on your needle).

If you have trouble casting on loosely enough, place the forefinger of your right hand on the needle in front of the stitch you've just cast on and place the next cast-on stitch on the other side of your finger. This helps create a small space between each cast-on stitch. It bears repeating that you can also cast on over both of your needles or over one of a larger size if your cast on is too tight.

For the cuffs of socks and other places where the cast on really has to stretch, see p. 123 for a decorative cast on developed for this very purpose.

CASTING ON MIDSTREAM
You may already know the next two cast on techniques, because they are sometimes used to begin a project. You'll need to know

at least one of them when you have to cast on stitches at the beginning or end of a row or in the middle of a row when your work is in progress—for example, casting on stitches in the middle of a row after they've been bound off in the previous row when you make a buttonhole, or casting on stitches at the beginning of a row for the body of a sweater that is knit cuff to cuff.

The knitted cast on
1. Make a slip knot on one needle and place it in your left hand. (Ignore this step if you already have stitches on the needle in your left hand.)

2. Knit a stitch (Figures 5 and 6), but do not remove the old stitch from the left needle.

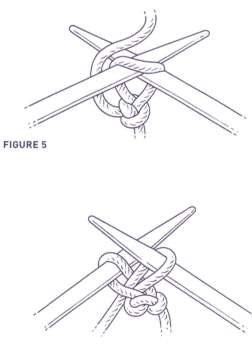

FIGURE 5

FIGURE 6

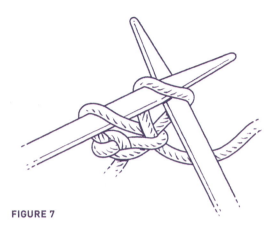

FIGURE 7

3. Slip the new knitted stitch from the right needle onto the left needle, carefully following Figure 7, as to how to mount it. (You can achieve a similar result by inserting the left-hand needle straight into the new stitch after you've created it and slipping it onto the left needle. It doesn't matter which method you use as long as you are consistent.) You now have one more stitch on the left-hand needle. Does the front loop of the new stitch look a little strange? Don't worry, it should.

4. Repeat Steps 2 and 3 until you've cast on all the required stitches. Please remember to cast on loosely if you're using this cast on at the bottom edge of a project.

How to Avoid Running Out of Yarn before You've Cast On All Your Stitches

If you're casting on a large number of stitches, there's a way to make sure you never run out of tail yarn. And you never want to run out of tail yarn, otherwise you'll need to rip out all the cast-on stitches, move the slip knot, and start again. This can be an incredible pain if you're casting on, say, 200 sts, and you run out of yarn after you've cast on 189 of them.

Using one end of each of two identical balls or both free ends of one ball, make a slip knot on your needle with both ends held together, leaving about a 6-in. tail (or more if you need to sew a seam). Then separate the two ends. Put one around your thumb and the other around your index finger. Follow the instructions for the long-tail cast on, but don't count the slip knot as a cast-on stitch. After you've cast on the required stitches, cut one of the pieces of yarn (leaving a 6-in. tail) and continue with the other. When you come back to the slip knot at the end of the first row or round, slip it off the needle and gently unravel it. Yes, we know you have two more tails to weave in, but trust us, it's worth it because you can't run out of yarn when you're using at least half of a ball to cast on with.

The cable cast on

If you're casting on to begin or to add to a piece of knitting and the edge formed by the knitted cast on is not firm enough, try the cable cast on. This cast on can also be used in the middle of a row.

If you are beginning your project, follow the instructions and illustrations for the knitted cast on until you have 2 sts on the left-hand needle. If you're adding onto existing stitches, start with the next sentence. Put your right-hand needle under the left needle and between the last 2 sts, wrap the yarn around it (Figure 8), and proceed to knit the stitch and place it on the left needle, just like the knitted cast on. Repeat until you have the number of stitches you need. Does the last stitch you cast on in this way look strange? That's okay, it always does.

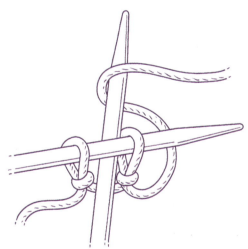

FIGURE 8

The provisional cast on

The provisional cast on is used for patterns that require you to come back to the cast-on stitches and knit them in the opposite direction. These cast-on loops are an example of live stitches (because you need to work

Knitting Together

We were once hired to knit a very long scarf in a very short time for a photo shoot. There was no way that either of us could knit the scarf alone, so Ahza started with the provisional cast on and, as soon as she could, Marion picked up the loops from the cast on and began to knit in the other direction. Together (and we mean *together*), we finished the scarf in record time.

them again). When will you use this cast on? Lace scarves are made truly symmetrical by starting in the middle and knitting to each end. Some sweater patterns ask that you knit a ruffle or lace pattern onto the cast-on row at the bottom of the garment. Also, you will find this technique useful if you have to change the length of a garment after you've knitted it.

Luckily, it is easier to work the provisional cast on than to explain its uses. It's identical to the long-tail cast on with two balls of yarn (see p. 26), but instead of using two balls of the same yarn, replace one ball with a suitable length of waste yarn (at least four times the width of your cast-on row). The waste yarn should be of a similar weight but a very different color. It's best if it's slippery or tightly twisted because you're going to remove it later on and you don't want it to leave little hairs behind.

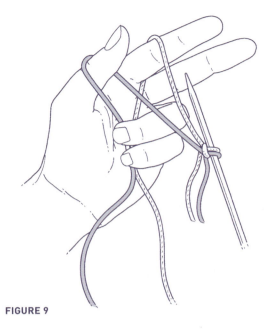

FIGURE 9

Make a slip knot with both yarns and place it on the right-hand needle. The waste yarn goes around your thumb and the yarn you will continue to use around the first finger (Figure 9). Continue as for the long-tail cast on. As you cast on, you'll notice that the waste yarn stays under the needle. The loops on your needle should be the yarn that you're going to continue with (Figure 10). If

a loop looks like it's made of waste yarn, you'll have to pull off all the stitches you've made since, including the offending one, and then continue casting on from that point. Don't forget to cast on an extra stitch so you will have the correct count when you take off the slip knot at the end of the first row.

When it's time to pick up stitches from the cast-on row, begin at the end where you cast on your first stitch. Carefully undo the waste yarn and, as you unravel it, a loop of the yarn you've been using will appear. Put this loop on your free needle right after you remove the waste yarn, then unpick more of the waste yarn until the next loop appears and put it on the same needles. If you like to knit dangerously, you can cut out the waste yarn, but be very, very careful. When all of the loops have been picked up, you should have the same number as the number of stitches you cast on. You're ready to begin the instructions for the new stitches.

I'm casting on in the round; how do I join my knitting?

After you've cast on all the stitches you need, make very, very sure that the bottom edge of the cast-on stitches is facing the center of the circle formed by the circular needle. Slip the

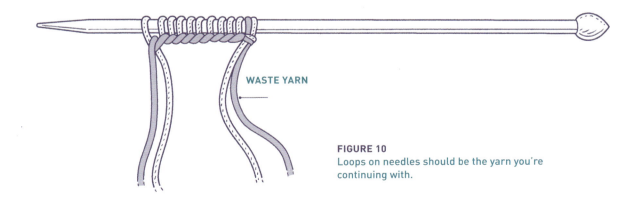

WASTE YARN

FIGURE 10
Loops on needles should be the yarn you're continuing with.

last stitch that you cast on onto the left point, where it will sit next to the first stitch that you cast on. Then, with the point that's in your right hand, slip the second stitch on the left needle (the first cast-on stitch) up and over the stitch you just moved and onto the right needle (Figure 11). Begin the first round by placing a marker and knitting the first stitch on the left needle. Joining in this way not only prevents a jog at the beginning of circular knitting, but it keeps your stitches from twisting at the last moment when you join them.

I twisted the cast-on row. How do I fix it?
If the cast-on row is twisted when you join the first round, you'll find yourself knitting a Möbius strip. Unless this is your intention, you'll have to unravel or unknit back to the join and start again. If you find this happening again and again, and you suspect that the stitches are twisting to thwart you, knit the first two or three rounds back and forth as rows. It's almost impossible to twist if you join after working several rows. Join these few rows with a seam as part of the finishing process.

How do I cast on onto double-pointed needles?
Cast on all of your stitches onto one of the needles, then slip the extra stitches from the ends of this needle onto two or three other needles. If your pattern doesn't tell you how to distribute the stitches, place an equal number on each needle. Being careful not to twist the stitches, join into a round in the same fashion as for a circular needle (Figure 12). After the stitches are joined, pick up another needle and knit across the needle that holds the last cast-on stitch and the ones that you've cast on first. When you finish these stitches, you will have a free needle to knit across the stitches on the next needle, and so on. Make sure you're always knitting the stitches on the needle to the left of the one that ends with the working yarn.

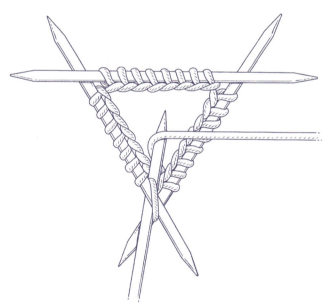

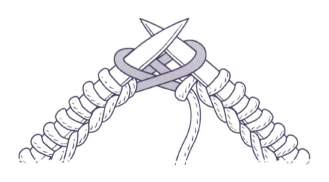

FIGURE 11
1. Slip the last cast-on stitch onto the left needle.
2. Slip the first cast-on stitch up and over that stitch, onto the right needle.

FIGURE 12
Cast-on stitches evenly distributed between double-pointed needles and ready to knit.

Don't Get Uptight with Your Bind Off

We'd feel remiss and unsymmetrical if we didn't add a word or two about binding off. We've found more than 20 ways to do it, but most are for decoration or special situations. There is only one bind off that you really need to know, and if you've ever finished a piece of knitting, you already know it. Just in case, we're including a refresher.

The bind off should end up being the same width as the piece you've just finished knitting. If you're like most of us, this means that you have to concentrate on binding off loosely. Why is this important to do? To avoid discovering that you can't get your newly knit sweater over your head because you bound off the neck too tightly.

Make sure you have enough yarn left in your ball, at least three times the width of your last row. Always bind off in pattern.

1. Work the first 2 sts of the last row.

2. Insert the point of the left needle into the front of the first stitch you knit (Figure 13), draw it over the second stitch you knit and over the point of the right needle (Figure 14), and release it (Figure 15).

3. Work another stitch. You will again have 2 sts on your right-hand needle.

4. Repeat Steps 2 and 3 until you have only 1 st on the right needle.

5. Cut the yarn (leaving the mandatory 6-in. tail) and pull the end through the last stitch to secure it.

If you find your bind off is too tight, use a larger needle in your right hand. If it's too loose take out the bind-off row and try again.

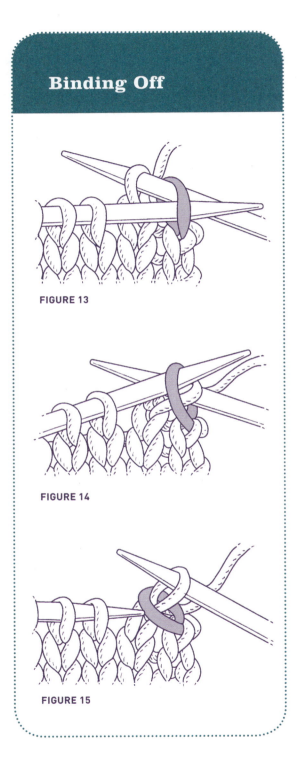

Binding Off

FIGURE 13

FIGURE 14

FIGURE 15

The Secret Language of Knitting Patterns

A lot of knitters say they absolutely cannot understand how to read a pattern. If you are one of them or are a knitter who has never read a pattern, this is the chapter for you. Here we give you a heads-up on how to choose a pattern, simple techniques you can use to make a pattern fit the person it's intended for, plus all the important extra stuff that patterns don't bother to tell you.

One of the biggest problems with reading knitting patterns is that there is no standard reference manual for the designers who write them. Because of that, each pattern or each company's patterns has its own internal logic (well, actually, you hope that it does).

The Craft Yarn Council of America (CYCA), whose members include many of the well-known knitting magazines and book publishers, has been working on providing a standard for pattern writing as well as everything else that has to do with knitting and crochet. We refer to their website (www.yarnstandards.com) often, and we thank them from the tips of our needles. The advent of knitting software has also helped standardize abbreviations and processes. Knitting magazines and publishers use computer programs ever more frequently. The software that professional designers use is very expensive, but there are less-expensive programs for knitters.

Increasing the Odds for Success: Picking a Pattern That Works

You want to give your intended pattern a pretty thorough examination before committing several months of your knitting life to it. Here are our three rules of pattern selection.

1. Get the picture

Pick a pattern with a photograph. And not just any photograph. What you want, in a perfect knitting world, is a straight-on shot of your garment that clearly shows its design elements. For a sweater, for example, the photo should show the neckline, the sleeves and how they join at the shoulders, and how the sweater is going to hang. It's a bonus if there's a side view as well. If the model is in violent motion—squatting, turning

Lost in Translation

Vintage patterns, patterns from the U.K., and those translated from other languages are not the best choices for beginners but are fine for knitters with previous pattern-reading experience. If you travel a lot and can't resist picking up patterns in other languages, search the Web for translations of knitting terms into American English. If not, track down a copy of *Knitting Languages* by Margaret Heathman, which translates to and from almost every language you can think of, including Croatian.

away coquettishly, or otherwise behaving in an artistic fashion—beware. The picture may be hiding flaws in the design that will become apparent only as you are knitting. And there's nothing more irritating than liking the overall design of a sweater but having no idea how the neck looks because the only photo has the model gazing at you over her shoulder. Even if the garment looks great in the photo, be aware that it may be pinned or otherwise adjusted (somewhere where you can't see it, of course) to make it fit the model. Finally, keep in mind that only a blessed few of us are built like models. And that leads us to the next tenet of pattern selection.

2. Honesty is the best policy

Compare your body to the picture of the pattern. It's truly a tragedy to spend hours and hours of your precious knitting time making something that is not suited to your figure. If you never buy sweaters with horizontal stripes because you don't like the way they make you look, you won't like the style any better if you knit the stripes yourself.

3. Don't bite off more than you can knit

A pattern with cables galore is not an appropriate choice for the cable novice, unless you have the patience of a saint. Argyle socks are not for a beginner. If you've never knitted with more than one color, making a Fair Isle vest may reduce you to tears or, worse, cause you to throw down your knitting and never pick it up again.

To help you choose a project for your skill level, almost every pattern written recently has a code indicating how experienced you need to be to knit it. This may take the form of a line of boxes—the more boxes that are filled in, the more difficult the pattern.

If you don't see little boxes, look near the title of the pattern. We hope you'll see a word like *beginner, intermediate,* or *experienced* or some other indication of the level of expertise required. Sometimes you have to dig a little deeper into the pattern to find a relevant word, or you'll have to deduce the skill level by looking at the photograph or reading parts of the pattern.

If you want to learn new knitting skills, we suggest one per pattern. Remember that knitting is supposed to be fun and relaxing. A frustrated knitter knits nothing.

Hoping It Will Fit Won't Necessarily Make It So

Some knitters just knit the pattern as written and wait to see what they end up with. Unfortunately, such knitters are often disappointed with the results. We'll show you how to adjust a simple pattern so you won't have to be one of those who knit in the dark.

If possible, find a similar garment that fits the intended recipient well. Take all the measurements from this garment that correspond to the finished measurements given in your pattern. If the measurements match those for the size you intend to knit, the garment should fit. If they don't, it probably won't, especially if you didn't make a gauge swatch (see p. 8).

So now what? Well, you've got a few options that don't require substantive pattern math.

- **Split the difference:** If your measurements fall between two sizes, read the larger and smaller size instructions carefully. Maybe you can just split the difference between the two sizes and use those numbers.

- **Don't worry about it:** How well does this sweater need to fit? Does the picture or schematic show a loose-fitting garment? Compare the measurements again. "Finished measurements" given in the pattern are usually an inch or two larger than the

---

DETERMINING THE SKILL LEVEL OF A PATTERN

Symbol	Level
▰▱▱▱	Beginner
▰▰▱▱	Easy
▰▰▰▱	Intermediate
▰▰▰▰	Experienced

actual body inside them. Maybe your version could be a touch less or a touch more loose fitting, and you wouldn't have to change a thing.

- **The secret needle trick:** Hardly anyone will admit to this—and certainly don't tell anyone we told you—but often going up or down a needle size or two (after you've made gauge) may do the trick.

- **Plan on losing 10 pounds before you finish knitting the sweater.**

BITING THE BULLET, OR HOW TO ADJUST A PATTERN FOR SIZE

There's a lot that can be done with pencil and paper, using simple math (*this* is why you took math in high school). And such steps can make the difference between a garment that fits well and one that looks as if it were knit by or for a kangaroo.

For an example, let's choose a pattern for a boat neck, dropped-sleeve sweater. This sweater has a schematic (a line drawing of all the pieces), thank goodness. Your gauge matches the gauge given in the pattern: 4 sts to 1 in. and 6 rows to 1 in.

Gather together the following materials:

- **Pencil (with eraser)**

- **Scratch paper**

- **Calculator**
  This is optional but extremely helpful.

- **Graph paper**
  If you want to make a schematic by hand.

- **Your measurements taken from a comparable garment**

- **One copy of the pattern with all the measurements you need to adjust highlighted**

Don't Try to Adjust a Pattern If . . .

- The size you want is greater than one size smaller or larger than the pattern. For example, let's say you find a sweater pattern written for S (42-in. chest), M (44-in. chest), L (46-in. chest), and XL (48-in. chest). Don't use it if the desired chest size is less than 40 in. (the difference between the S and M sizes subtracted from the S size) or more than 50 in. (the difference between the L and XL sizes added to the XL size). Why? Because the overall proportions begin to change. A person doesn't get shorter and shorter as he or she gets thinner.
- The stitch pattern is very complicated and/or made up of large horizontal or vertical repeats. It is possible to adjust these patterns, but you need a good deal of experience to do it.

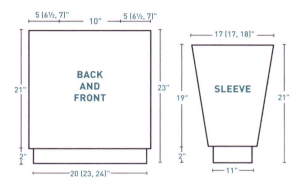

Original sweater schematic showing three sizes.

- **At least one more copy of the pattern**
  You're going to write your adjustments on this.

- **The pattern schematic (line drawing) with measurements**
  If your pattern doesn't have a schematic, you can draw one by using the pattern instructions and graph paper. Although a schematic is not required, it helps to see where you're going and reveals obvious mistakes.

- **A copy of the schematic without the measurements**
  You can make this copy by tracing the original schematic under a very bright light or against a window, omitting the numbers.

Place the original knitting instructions and schematics and the copies you will mark up with new instructions and measurements side by side. Write the desired measurements on the blank schematic.

Changes in width (circumference)
Our pattern says, *"For Back and Front (make 2): Cast on 80 sts. Knit 12 rows in k1, p1 ribbing, then continue in stockinette until piece measures 23 in. Bind off all stitches."* The smallest pattern

width is shown to be 20 in. on the original schematic, but you want it to be 19 in. How many stitches should you cast on?

Divide the number of stitches in the original pattern by your stitch gauge.

80 (number of cast-on sts from original pattern) ÷ 4 (sts per inch) = 20 in.

You want the sweater to be 38 in. around or 19 in. across each piece.

19 in. x 4 (sts per inch) = 76 (number of sts to cast on)

In a more complicated pattern, this would be a good time to check for any other numbers that refer to circumference or width. Adjust those numbers and write them on the new pattern.

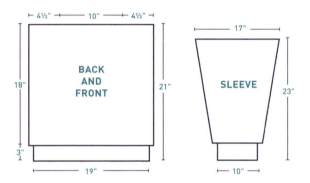

Schematic with the new numbers written in.

Changes in length
When the length is given as a measurement (such as inches), simply change the measurement to the one that you want. Our pattern says, *"Continue in stockinette stitch until the piece measures 23 in. from the beginning, then bind off."* You want your sweater to measure 21 in. from cast on to bind off. Replace 23 in. with 21 in.

If the length is given in rows, divide the number of rows by the row gauge to get the length in inches. If you need a different length, multiply the number of inches that you want by your row gauge. In our pattern, it says, *"Work in k1, p1 ribbing for 12 rows."* You want the ribbing to be 3 in. long.

12 (rows) ÷ 6 (rows per inch) = 2 in. (length of original pattern's ribbing)

You'll need to add more rows to get a 3-in. ribbing.

3 in. x 6 (rows per inch) = 18 rows (length of desired ribbing)

Change the vertical measurements and note them on the new schematic. Your adjusted pattern will read, *"For Back and Front (make 2): Cast on 76 sts. Work 18 rows in k1, p1 ribbing, then continue in stockinette until piece measures 21 in. from beginning. Bind off all stitches."*

Changing length and width when increases are involved

Our pattern reads: *"Sleeve (make 2): Cast on 44 sts. Work 12 rows in k1, p1 ribbing. Changing to stockinette st, work 6 rows more, increasing 1 st at each side on next row and every 6th row thereafter for a total of 12 times (68 sts). Work even until sleeve measures 21 in. from beginning. Bind off."*

You want to replace the rows of ribbing with stockinette for rolled-bottom sleeves, so the sleeves will need to be one inch tighter at the wrist. Also, you want to make the sleeves 2 in. longer, while keeping the same number of stitches at the top of the sleeve. It's easier than you think. Just take it step by step.

You've already learned how to change circumference and length, so start by making those changes and writing them on the new schematic. Here's the new pattern with the

information that you've figured out and blank spaces for what you don't know yet: *"Sleeve (make 2): Cast on 40 sts. Work 18 rows in stockinette st, then inc 1 st at each side on next row and every __th row thereafter for a total of __ times (68 sts). Work even until sleeve measures 23 in. from beginning. Bind off."*

What's left to do? Figure out the number of stitches you need to increase to get from the cast-on to the bind-off rows and how to space the increase rows. First, figure out the total number of stitches you need to increase by subtracting the number of cast-on stitches from the number you bind off.

68 (number of sts to bind off) – 40 (number of sts to cast on) = 28 (total number of sts to be increased)

Divide the result by the number of increases in each row to get the number of times you will be increasing.

In this case, because each time you increase, you increase 1 st on each side of the sleeve, divide the total number of increases by 2.

28 (sts to increase) ÷ 2 (increases in 1 row) = 14 (increase rows)

Figure out the total number of rows of the new sleeve by multiplying the length you want by the row gauge.

23 (new length in inches) x 6 (rows per inch) = 138 (rows in new sleeve length)

Subtract the 18 rows that you knit to replace the ribbing to get 120 rows in the new sleeve.

Divide the total number of rows remaining in the sleeve by the number of times you need to increase. The result will be the number of rows in each increase repeat.

120 (total rows) ÷ 14 (increase rows) = 8.57 (rows in each repeat)

Now, 8.57 rows in each increase repeat looks a little strange, doesn't it? Round the number of rows in each repeat down to the nearest even number. Then compare this number to the total number of rows and decide where to put the extra rows. In our case, 8.57 rounds down to 8.

Multiply the rows in each increase by the number of increases:

8 x 14 = 112

Add an extra row before the first increase row so that you'll always increase on the knit side:

112 + 1 = 113

You have 7 rows left to knit after the last increase for a total length of 138 rows.

Here, at long last, are the new sleeve instructions: *"Sleeve (make 2): Cast on 40 sts. Work 18 rows in stockinette st. Then increase 1 st at each side of next row and every 8th row thereafter for a total of 14 times (68 sts). Work even until sleeve measures 23 in. from beginning. Bind off."*

Victory! You have just adjusted a pattern to fit. The sweater body is shorter and it has more ribbing at the bottom. You've changed the sleeve length and even its shape! Give yourself a pat on the back. Knit on with confidence knowing that you can always adjust a pattern to fit.

The smallest size of the pattern for my sweater is too big. What should I do?
The principles and how to apply them also hold true when you want to make something smaller. However, you might want to write out the steps as you work through them so you don't become confused.

ADJUSTING A PATTERN FOR GAUGE
If you have found a yarn that you absolutely, positively love and you've found the perfect pattern to use with it but you can't match the gauge no matter what you do, it's possible to adjust the pattern to reflect your desired gauge.

Adjusting a Pattern for Both Size and Gauge

If you want to change both size and gauge, think three times about whether it's worth it and then consider whether you've become a knitting masochist. Frankly, we would not attempt this unless you let us use knitting software or threatened to hold our favorite needles to the fire. There are so many wonderful patterns in this world and so little time in which to knit them, that to pick one that would require this kind of mathematical gymnastics would make your knitting life unnecessarily frustrating (in our opinion).

We trust you've already considered how the qualities of the yarn will affect the pattern. If you have selected a different type of yarn as well as a different size, the result will look different. Think of a silk sweater that drapes over every curve versus one knit from a chunky yarn that conceals more than it reveals. If you still want to proceed, gauge adjustment is for the detail oriented.

Use the pattern alteration techniques we outlined earlier in this chapter. However, changing both the number of stitches to the inch and rows to the inch in a pattern is time-consuming. (That's why patterns advise you to change your needle size if you don't make gauge.) You will need to look at every instruction in the pattern and consider whether it needs to be changed to reflect the new gauge (it usually does). Go slowly and carefully and check your work often. Remembering how to do ratios is very helpful. After you've finished, check everything over once again and proceed with caution. If you're careful, you'll end up with the sweater of your dreams.

Don't Even Think of Doing It!

Except for your own use, it's illegal to make copies of copyrighted patterns. If you do so, you're denying the author the royalties that he or she would otherwise receive from the sale of that book or pattern. Please don't do it.

AVOIDING THE MOTHER OF ALL EMERGENCIES: LOSING THE PATTERN

Okay, you've selected your pattern and you've made any necessary adjustments to it. Before you begin knitting, make several copies of the pattern *for your own use only*. Keep at least one extra copy where you know you can find it, should you lose the original or need extra copies. Keep another with your project. On this copy, highlight the information that pertains to the size you are knitting. On the schematic of the different garment pieces, highlight the measurements for your size. If the pattern includes a chart, clearly outline the portion that pertains to your size. Mark this copy up as much as you like. We make notations of our changes on this copy and keep it so we can duplicate our work again if we want to.

Knitting as a Second Language

Because of space considerations, which are partly for the knitter's benefit (if patterns take up less space, there can be more patterns in the same book or magazine), patterns increasingly rely on abbreviations, a punctuation-powered shorthand notation, and a sometimes vague or confusing vocabulary.

What do I do if I have no idea what a particular abbreviation means?

If the key for a particular abbreviation isn't in the pattern, search through the pattern book—any collection worth its salt is going to provide you with an abbreviation key *somewhere*. If you find you're out of luck on that front, we offer you a secret decoder ring, and it's in "Abbreviations: A Magic Decoder" on p. 153.

If you can't find the abbreviation you need there, go to www.yarnstandards.com for their list. If that doesn't yield an answer, try the largest magic decoder ring of all, the Internet. If you're skeptical, just type "k2tog" into your search engine and see what happens.

Where are the instructions for actually knitting this pattern?

This is often a great mystery, especially for first-time pattern readers. Look for the words "Cast on" or "Row/Round 1" after the information section that begins every pattern. The pattern information above the first row is worth reading. It tells you everything you need to have or know before you start knitting. Here's some of the information you'll find in most patterns that we think deserves special mention.

Garment sizes

Pay attention to finished measurements because they determine the ultimate fit and/or size of what you make. They are usually an inch or two larger than body measurements so your finished garment won't end up skintight once you join the pieces together. Alternatively, this information is often presented on the schematic of the various pieces of the garment.

Gauge

Rest assured that if your gauge doesn't match that of the pattern writer's, the finished measurements of the garment won't match those of the pattern, and whatever you're making will be a different size and shape than you hoped. Please read "Always Make a Gauge Swatch Before You Begin a Project" on p. 8 if you've forgotten how to make one.

Abbreviations

If you're lucky, the pattern will include a list of the abbreviations used and their meanings. Otherwise, check out our chart on p. 153.

Special stitches

Many patterns offer an explanation of the special stitches used in the project. If you're making a popcorn-stitch sweater, you hope the pattern will explain how to make popcorn stitches, so you don't have to go running to a reference book to figure it out.

What's this right side, left side, right side, wrong side business?

Patterns can use almost the same terms with different meanings. The use of *right*, as in "right side facing," "on the right-hand side," or "after a right-side row," causes the most confusion. Is this a plot to drive you round the bend? No. Actually, the pattern is trying to be precise.

- *Right* is often used in conjunction with left. In such a case, the reference, most of the time, is to the right-hand side of the garment when you are wearing it.

- *Right* is also used in conjunction with wrong as in "right side" and "wrong side." In almost all patterns, the right side is the side that faces out, or the public side, and the wrong side refers to the side next to your skin, or the private side. To eliminate this particular confusion, we use the words *public* and *private* in this book.

It can be confusing when a pattern that is knitted back and forth in rows says "ending with a wrong-side row" or "ending with a right-side row" and then continues with a new set of directions. The designer is saying, "After you finish working this row (and I'm checking with you to make sure that you have ended with the correct row), turn your work around and begin the next set of directions." In other words, to end with a wrong-side row means to work that wrong-side row; to end with a right-side row means to work that right-side row, and then to proceed as instructed.

How many times do I have to repeat these instructions?

Pattern repeats can make even experienced knitters weep. To avoid any misunderstanding, put your speed-reading skills on the shelf and read the repeat instructions very, very carefully, bit by bit, paying special attention to the punctuation.

- A *period* (.) ends a sequence of instructions. It often comes at the end of each row or round and sometimes within it.

- A *comma* (,) separates one instruction from the next in a set of instructions.

- *Parentheses* ( ) are used to enclose various choices for the knitter. An example of this is to enclose the stitch counts of the different sizes for which the pattern is written—for instance, "For S (M, L) cast on 60 (70, 80) sts." In repeats, parentheses are used to set off a set of instructions that will be repeated: "(K1, p2) until you reach the first marker."

- *Brackets* [ ] are used in the same way as parentheses and, more important, alternate with parentheses to nest one instruction inside of another. So, "([K1, p2] 3 times, k6) until you reach the end of the row" means, repeat k1, p2 three times, then k6, then continue to repeat the entire sequence until you get to the end of the row.

- *Asterisks* (*) when used in pairs have the same meaning as parentheses. But sometimes only one asterisk is used at the beginning of a repeat and the one at the end is left off. In these cases, the number of times to repeat the sequence comes right after the end of the stitches contained in the repeat. For example, "*K5, p4, repeat from * 3 times" means k5, p4, k5, p4, k5, p4. But, "*K5, p4, repeat from * 3 times *more*" means k5, p4, k5, p4, k5, p4, k5, p4. Make sure you understand how many times to repeat an instruction or set of instructions. If you don't pay careful attention to the repeats, you may end up using all the stitches on your needle before you get to the end of the instructions for that row, or you may get to the end of the instructions for the row and find you have stitches hanging out on your left needle waiting to be used.

What a Difference a Word Makes

The use of *twice* or × 2 or *2* after parentheses, brackets, or asterisks means to execute whatever is within them a total of two times. However, if the pattern says *twice more* or *2 times more*, you'd execute the same instructions three times.

Managing Your Repeats

In a pattern particularly loaded with repeats, you may want to use stitch markers of different colors to mark off groups of stitches. In the example given in the text—"K3, * k2 [(yo, k2tog) × 2, k2] repeat between [ ] 2 times more*; then repeat from * to* 2 (3, 4) times more, k3—we'd use one color for the overall paired asterisk repeat, a second color for the brackets, and a third color for the parentheses, if necessary.

If you don't use markers, count your stitches at the end of each row or two to keep your knitting in line with the pattern directions. Or, if achieving the correct stitch count is giving you agita, you can write out the row (or round) in long hand, literally writing out all of the repeats. This way is the most time-consuming but also the surest.

Okay, let's see if you're ready to be road tested. Here's an example stuffed full of repeats and options. If you can figure out the total number of stitches for even one of the sizes, you get a gold star: "K3, *k2 [(yo, k2tog) x 2, k2] repeat between [ ] 2 times more*; then repeat from * to* 2 (3, 4) times more, k3. __ (__, __ sts).

It is hoped that, in a complicated pattern, the designer will include the total number of stitches that you should have after you end the row. If so, offer up a special blessing to him or her. If not, you might want to figure the number out for yourself and make note of it on your pattern for easy reference. And by the way, the stitch totals for our example are 66 (86, 106).

How do I read a chart?
Charts are used to avoid having to write out the directions for each row, either because they'd be too confusing or because they'd take up too much space. They are often found in color work and can also be used to help you follow elaborate stitch patterns, such as traveling cables and lace knitting.

Once you understand the basics, you may find a chart easier to follow than long rows filled with confusing instructions. Because they are visual, you don't have to know the language the pattern is written in; but, and this is a big *but*, chart symbols aren't standardized. "A Sample Color Chart" on p. 44, will help you understand the principles.

The key to knitting from charts is "The Key." In a color chart, the key tells you what color to use in each square of the chart. In a chart with different stitches, it tells you what stitch to use by assigning a different symbol to each stitch. And if the pattern has several colors and different stitches, there are charts for that too.

A Sample Color Chart

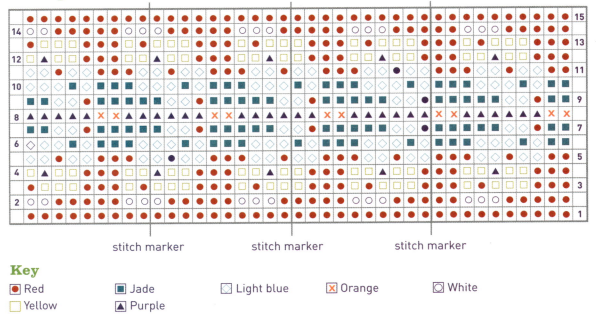

stitch marker   stitch marker   stitch marker

Key

● Red   ■ Jade   ◇ Light blue   ✕ Orange   ○ White

□ Yellow   ▲ Purple

Before starting to knit from a chart, make sure you understand the key because:

- Chart symbols aren't standardized.

- There can be two symbols for the same stitch, depending on whether you're working on the public side or the private side.

- The same symbol can be used for two different stitches, so you'll need to know what row you're working to know what stitch to use.

- One row in a chart sometimes represents two rows of knitting.

- Sometimes there are blank spaces in a chart that don't represent a stitch. Usually these blank spaces are filled in with black.

If a chart has several sizes indicated (you'll find notations such as "For small, start here" and "For medium, start here"), take a highlighter and mark the size you'll be knitting.

If you're knitting back and forth

Read the chart exactly as you knit in rows. Unless the pattern tells you otherwise, start with the bottom right square of the chart and work left across the bottom row. Begin the second row one square up and knit from left to right. This represents turning your knitting and working on the private side. Now you're back at the right side of the chart. Move up one square and work from right to left for the third row, and so on. Kind pattern writers number the rows of the charts, odd numbers on the right and even numbers on the left.

If you're knitting in the round

Read the chart exactly as you knit in the round. Read the first row of the chart from right to left, starting with the first square (which represents your first stitch). After you finish knitting across the first row of the chart, you're ready to knit the first stitch in the next round. This stitch is above the first stitch in the previous round so, on the chart, the matching square is above the one you used for the first stitch. As you may have guessed, it's the first square in the second row on the *right-hand* side of the chart. Continue up the chart, *always* reading from right to left.

Keeping track of where you are in your chart

Position a straightedge on the chart immediately above the row that you'll be knitting next and secure it with masking tape. Move the straightedge up when you finish the row. The row below the one you're working on represents the stitches that you now have on your needle, so it's easier to tell where you are and to find mistakes early. The other option is to buy a roll of transparent removable highlighter tape and place it over the row you are knitting. Sometimes this tape can be found in knitting stores, and it's also found in office supply stores.

If your row or round has lots of stitches, you can keep track of where you are by drawing vertical colored pencil lines at fixed intervals. (On the chart on p. 44, note the heavy line after every 10 sts.) Place stitch markers that match the pencil colors on your needle at the same stitch intervals (every 30 sts or whatever works for you and your pattern). You'll find your place easily; and if you make a mistake, you'll know it by the time you reect the next stitch marker, not several rows later.

What if the pattern instructions still don't make sense?

Some patterns are hard to understand, especially if they're translated from another

A Cautionary Tale in Pattern Reading

Flora called in a panic. She was making a sweater for her husband. It was a raglan sweater, knit from the bottom up on a circular needle. As she was knitting up toward the neck, she saw with dismay that while one sleeve seemed to be correctly located at the side of the sweater, the other was coming out of the middle of the chest!

When she brought the sweater over, we could see that she had not divided the stitches exactly as the pattern had directed on the row that joined the sleeves to the body. Because the instructions didn't make sense to her, she did what she thought was logical. She should have had a little more faith in the instructions, even though they seemed odd, to say the least.

We unraveled the sweater just past the offending sleeve, redivided the front, back, and sleeve stitches, and got her back on track with the sleeves happily at their respective sides.

language. The good news is that the more often you knit and follow patterns, the better you'll become at deciphering them. If you really find yourself in a jam, shaking your head and saying this can't be possible, just start again, reading and knitting the offending passage one instruction at a time. Or try writing out that part of the pattern without the abbreviations. Sometimes it helps to write each row on a separate index card. Try executing it, paying special attention to the punctuation. If it still doesn't seem right or sensible to you, try it anyway for a few rows and see what happens. (See Flora's cautionary tale on p. 45.)

Occasionally patterns can be published with mistakes and/or omissions in the directions. If your pattern has been written recently, check the publisher's website for corrections. If you don't find help from the publisher's website, go to Ravelry (www.ravelry.com). It's a great resource because the chances are that many knitters have already made this pattern and you can read through their comments to find out if they found this mistake and how they corrected it. If you still can't find corrections, set the project aside for a day or so, then come back and try it again with fresh eyes. As you knit from more patterns, you'll begin to know earlier and earlier when something is wrong.

Really smart knitters check for corrections before they begin. You can save yourself a lot of heartache (not to mention knitting and reknitting).

Getting Rid of the Stair-Step Phenomenon

Your pattern will likely begin a row with the instruction "Decrease (or increase) at each end of the row."

When a decrease or increase is made in the first or last stitch of the row, it will appear as a stair step on each side, which can lead to finishing difficulties later on, so most patterns will tell you specifically if they actually want you to do this. General Knitting Knowledge assumes that you already know when to use what is known as a full-fashion decrease or increase, which will give you a smoother edge. To do this, work one or two stitches in the pattern at the beginning of the row before you decrease or increase, then decrease or increase. If you need to decrease or increase at the end of that row as well, make sure you position it so you have the same number of stitches in from the end of the row as you have in the beginning.

Who Says It's General Knitting Knowledge?

We don't know who assumes that some things are "General Knitting Knowledge," but we'd like to have a word with him or her. How this works is that the pattern designer or editor assumes the knitter has a certain level of knowledge. Patterns generated by knitting software assume that we all know how to do everything—very flattering but often not the case. The result is unspecific directions and/or the use of terminology that's unfamiliar to the reader. Let's go over the worst offenders in the order in which you might encounter them in a pattern. We'll fill you in on the General Knitting Knowledge you might not be familiar with.

My pattern doesn't say what cast on to use; does it matter?

Well, actually, yes it can, depending on how firm an edge you want. But almost without exception a pattern is simply going to tell you to cast on a certain number of stitches, and that's it. For more on this topic, see p. 24.

My pattern doesn't say what kind of increase or decrease to use; does it matter?

Again, it depends. If you're increasing a number of stitches across a row after your ribbed waistband, no, it doesn't matter. And if you're working in garter stitch, it doesn't matter because the increases or decreases won't show on the public side of the work.

But if you're working in stockinette and increasing at the beginning and end of a row as you knit a sleeve, or decreasing at the beginning and end of a row to shape the armholes of a sweater, or working the V in a V-neckline, it does matter. Why? Because, depending on the decrease you choose, it will either slant right or slant left; this is also the case with certain increases. And when you have paired increases and decreases, whether they slant inward (/ \) or outward (\ /), they have a particular look. Unfortunately, many pattern writers assume that you know which look is best for that pattern and how to make it happen. With increases, there is the added consideration of how big a hole the increase may leave in the fabric.

If you learn increases and decreases in relation to the way they look rather than where you place them in the row or round, you'll always know which one to use. So what follows is a short primer of right-slanting and left-slanting increases and decreases for you to make merry with.

It's customary for decreases or increases to be made only on the public (right) side of the garment, but there will be cases in which you'll need to make them on the private side, so you need to know how to make right- and left-slanting increases and decreases in both knit and purl.

RIGHT-SLANTING DECREASES
Worked on the knit side (k2tog)

Knit the next 2 sts on the left needle together. Insert the point of the right needle, from front to back, into the *front loop* of the second stitch on the left needle and then the first (Figure 1). Finish the stitch as you would a knit stitch. Your right needle should point to the right when you insert it into the 2 sts. This will help you remember that the k2tog decrease slants right.

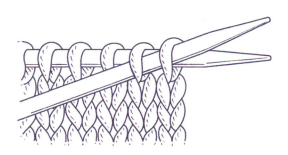

FIGURE 1
K2tog decrease, right slanting

Decreasing in Reverse Stockinette

In reverse stockinette, the purl side is the public side. In that case, use the purl equivalent of a right-slanting knit decrease to make a left-slanting decrease and the purl equivalent of the left-slanting knit decrease for a right slant.

Worked on the purl side (p2tog)

The purl equivalent is meant to slant to the right on the knit side of the work. Insert the point of the right needle into the first 2 sts on the left needle as if to purl (Figure 2), wrap the yarn around the needle as if to purl, and complete the stitch.

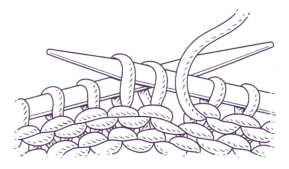

FIGURE 2
P2tog decrease, right slanting on the knit side

LEFT-SLANTING DECREASES

Worked on the knit side (k2togtbl)
Insert the point of the right needle, from front to back, through the *back loops* of the first 2 sts on the left needle (Figure 3) and finish as you would a knit stitch. The right needle should point to the left when you insert it into the 2 sts. This will help you remember that the k2togtbl decrease slants left.

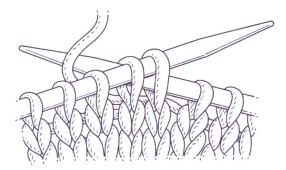

FIGURE 3
K2togtbl decrease, left slanting

Worked on the purl side (p2togtbl)
The purl equivalent slants to the left on the knit side of the work. Here's the easiest way that we've found. Slip the next 2 sts from the left needle to the right needle as if you were going to knit them, then slip them back onto the left needle through their *front loops*.

Working in the *back loops* of these 2 sts, insert the point of your right needle into the stitch farthest away from you and then into the first one, as shown in Figure 4. With the right needle under the left, purl the 2 sts together.

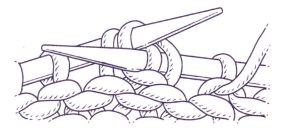

FIGURE 4
P2togtbl, left-slanting decrease on the knit side

THE MOST VISIBLE INCREASE

The most visible increase, called a yarn over (yo or yrn), is made by wrapping the yarn over the right needle before you work the next stitch. A yarn over creates a hole beneath it and is used as a design element in lace and other patterns and to make eyelets and small buttonholes. The result looks the same on either side of the fabric, but the way you wrap the yarn depends on the surrounding stitches.

Yarn over between knit stitches

Bring the yarn forward and over the top of the right needle and then to the back before you knit the next stitch on the left needle (Figure 5).

Yarn over between purl stitches

With the yarn in front of the needles, bring it over the top of the right needle so that the yarn is in the back, then bring it to the front again between the two needles (Figure 6) and purl the next stitch.

   A row or round containing yarn overs is most often followed by knitting or purling into the yarn over on the next row or round.

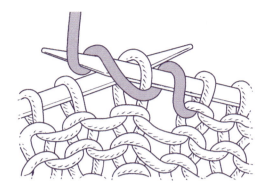

FIGURE 6
YO between purl stitches

THE LESS VISIBLE INCREASES

These increases are made into a single stitch instead of between 2 sts.

Knit into the front and back of the same stitch (kfb)

Knit the stitch, pulling the loop through onto the right needle but not taking the old stitch off the left needle (Figure 7). Swing the point of the right needle over the left one and knit into the back loop of the same stitch (Figure 8 on p. 50). Finally, slip the old stitch off the left needle.

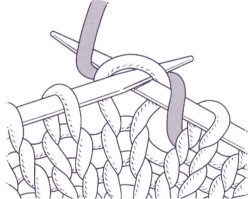

FIGURE 5
YO between knit stitches

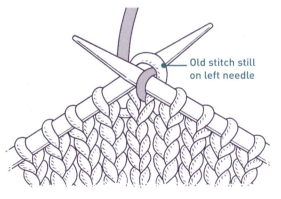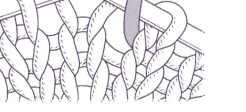

Old stitch still on left needle

FIGURE 7

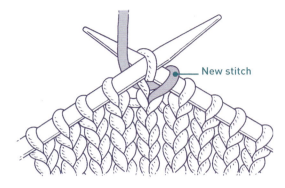

FIGURE 8

New stitch

Purl into the front and back of the same stitch (pfb)

If you are on a purl row, the process is the same as for a knit row. Purl the stitch, pulling the loop through to the right needle, but don't remove the old stitch from the left needle (Figure 9). Swing the point of the right needle over the left, enter the back loop from the left side, and purl it (Figure 10). Slip the old stitch off the left needle.

These two increases don't slant, nor do they leave a hole, but there is a bar below the second stitch of the increase. If you're knitting a garment with paired increases and you use either of these, be careful to leave one more stitch at the edge of the left side so that the bar will appear in the same position at both ends.

THE ALMOST INVISIBLE INCREASES

The increases described here are made between 2 sts, making them easy to position. We use these increases willy-nilly because we find the difference in the way that they slant insignificant. For the perfectionist, however, we've indicated the direction of their slight slant. The same abbreviation, m1 (for make 1), is used for all of the increases in this category. Be warned, though, that in patterns written in the U.K. or Canada, "m1" is a generic term used for all increases.

Before you begin these increases, pull your needles apart slightly and you will see a horizontal piece of yarn between the last stitch on the right needle and the first stitch on the left needle.

Right-slanting make 1
Between two knit stitches

Insert the tip of the left needle under the horizontal piece of yarn from back to front, making a new stitch on the left needle (Figure 11). Knit into the front loop of the new stitch (Figure 12). The stitch you've just made is twisted, preventing a hole.

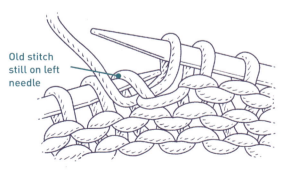

Old stitch still on left needle

FIGURE 9

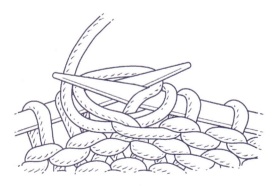

FIGURE 10

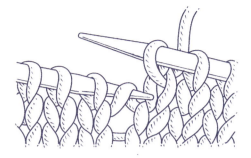

FIGURE 11
Right-slanting make 1 between knit stitches,
step 1

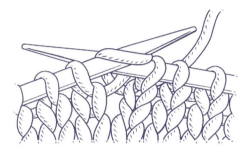

FIGURE 12
Right-slanting make 1 between knit stitches,
step 2

Between two purl stitches

Work like the knit increase just described,
purling into the front loop of the new stitch
(Figure 13).

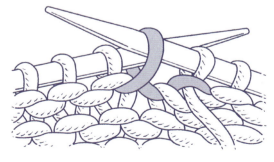

FIGURE 13
Right-slanting make 1 between purl stitches

Left-slanting make 1

Between two knit stitches

Insert the tip of the left needle under the
horizontal piece of yarn from front to back,
making a new loop on the left needle
(Figure 14). Knit into the back part of the
loop. The stitch you've just made is twisted,
preventing a hole (Figure 15).

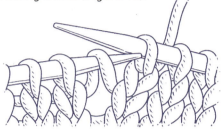

FIGURE 14
Left-slanting make 1 between knit stitches,
step 1

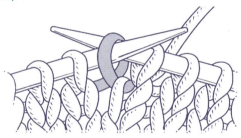

FIGURE 15
Left-slanting make 1 between knit stitches,
step 2

Between two purl stitches

Work as the knit stitch (just described), purling
into the back loop of the new stitch (Figure 16).

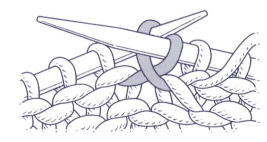

FIGURE 16
Left-slanting make 1 between purl stitches

DECREASING OR INCREASING EVENLY MANY TIMES IN THE SAME ROW

Sometimes the pattern will tell you to decrease (or increase) a specific number of stitches evenly in the same row but doesn't tell you where to place them. For example: "Decrease 6 sts evenly over 35 sts in next row."

The way of the perfectionist

Increasing and decreasing are handled in almost the same way, so you have to learn only one new skill. First, count the number of stitches you have on your needle. Divide the result by the total number of decreases or increases you're asked to make plus 1. Why plus 1? Because, if you divide the number of stitches by the number of decreases or increases, the last shaping will occur at the end of the row, creating a stair step. Place stitch markers on your needle after each group of stitches.

To continue with our earlier example ("Decrease 6 sts evenly over 35 sts in next row"), here's the math:

35 (sts) ÷ [6 (number of decreases) + 1] = 5 (number of sts between each marker)

- To decrease, use the stitches on each side of each marker to form the decreases. Remove the markers as you go. Written out, the instructions for this row would be: "*K4, (dec, k3) x 5, dec, k4 (29 sts)."

- To increase *between* the 2 sts surrounding a marker, m1 in the bar between them. Remove the marker. Written out, our example would be: "*K5, m1, repeat from * x 6, k5 (41 sts)."

Now, what if the math isn't tidy and even? In that case, you'll have to position the stitch markers to distribute the extra stitches as

evenly as possible. Say, for example, we'd started with 40 sts for our example:

40 ÷ (6 + 1) = 5 plus a remainder of 5 sts

Place the markers every 5 sts. To integrate those leftover 5 sts evenly over the seven intervals between markers, move the markers so you have added 1 st to five of the intervals. The written instructions for a decrease row might look like this: "K4, dec; k4, dec; k4, dec; k4, dec; k4, dec; k4, dec; k4 (34 sts)." For an increase row, it might look like this: "K5, inc, *k6, inc, repeat from * 4 more times, k5."

Too confusing? Here's another way. Write the number of stitches in each grouping on a line. Then adjust these numbers for the remainder. When the result is satisfactory, knit it.

Time-consuming? Yes. Is it worth the trouble? Yes, it is for the perfectionist or when design elements make it necessary to have absolutely equal spaces between the decreases or increases.

The way of the eyeball

Look at the row and place one stitch marker for each decrease or increase as evenly as you can throughout. Adjust the markers until you are satisfied that the spaces between them look even, then proceed, increasing between the markers or decreasing the stitches on each side of each marker.

What should I do when my pattern says to "reverse shaping"?

A pattern will sometimes give complete instructions for one side of a garment (the front left side of a cardigan, for example) but will tell you to work the other side (for example, the right side) as for first side, "reversing shaping." This saves pattern space but does nothing for your stress level, especially when you read these words for the first time.

Ahza's Beautiful Glove

We wish you could see the beautiful glove that Ahza has knitted. It's knit in two colors. The back has black stitches on a white ground, and the front has white and black vertical stripes. Each finger is outlined by one row of black stitches. It took Ahza a long time to knit and she keeps it in a special box, wrapped in tissue paper. Where is the other glove, you may ask? Alas, it was never made. The pattern directions for the second glove said, "Repeat for the left hand, reversing shaping." Too bad Ahza lost the pattern before she learned how to decode the words *reverse shaping*.

The most reliable solution is to write out your own instructions, row by row, for the piece whose instructions need to be reversed. Some things won't change, like the number of stitches to cast on, the total length of the piece, and so on. But make sure to replace all the parts of the pattern instructions that refer to a horizontal direction with its opposite. "End of row" will become "beginning of row" and a decrease that slanted to the left should be replaced with one that will slant to the right (see p. 47 for a primer on paired increases and decreases). After you've painstakingly written out the new instructions and checked them for accuracy and believability, knit from them.

The pattern just says to bind off; does it matter how I bind off—loosely, snugly, in pattern?
When binding off, it is crucial that the tension of the bind-off row match that of the rest of the knitted piece. If you bind off too tightly, the piece will draw in; if too loosely, it will spread out at the top. (If you need a refresher in how to bind off, see p. 32.) In some cases, like at the top of the shoulder, you can choose not to bind

off at all but to attach the piece to another as part of the finishing process (see p. 90).

What am I supposed to do when a pattern tells me to "pick up and knit"?
The pattern is telling you to pick up loops from an edge that has no live stitches and begin to knit them. When would you want to do this? To make a buttonhole band on the front of a cardigan, to add a turtleneck onto a sweater, or to turn the heel of a sock. You might also use it to join knitted pieces as you go rather than joining them together later on, as in patchwork knitting.

To pick up stitches from a cast-on or bound-off edge

With the right side facing you, place the tip of your right needle into the center of the first stitch under the cast-on or bind-off row on the right-hand side of the piece and wrap the yarn from a new ball over the right needle as if to knit. Draw the yarn through to complete the stitch and continue in this manner (Figure 1, p .54) until you have picked up the required number of stitches. (We don't have to remind you to leave a 6-in. tail for weaving in later, do we?)

If you're picking up from garter stitch, look for the row with Vs between the top 2 rows of bumps and pick up stitches from there.

It's most important that the stitches are evenly spaced when you pick them up. If you can't quite match the number indicated in the pattern, you can compensate by decreasing or increasing in the next couple of rows.

To pick up stitches from a side edge

If the right side is in stockinette, insert the tip of your needle into the corner stitch at the right-hand edge of your piece and wrap the yarn from the new ball around the needle as if to knit (Figure 2). Draw the yarn through to complete the stitch and repeat along the side of the knitting as directed, or until you reach the next corner. Because stockinette stitches are wider than they are tall, you must skip a row every few stitches. If you don't, you'll pick up too many stitches and the edge will flare. The usual ratio is to pick up 3 sts for every 4 rows (Figure 3). Adjust for the correct number of stitches as you pick them up.

If you're picking up stitches from a garter stitch edge, knit into every bump at the edge of the row.

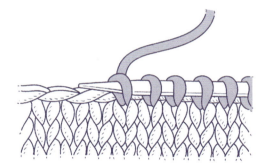

FIGURE 1
Several picked-up stitches

FIGURE 2
Picking up stitches from a side edge

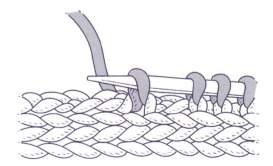

FIGURE 3

Picking up stitches from a curved edge

Fold the point where the curve begins to the point at which it ends. This crease marks the middle of the curve. Place a marker there (we use T-pins). Fold one end of the curve to the middle marker and put a marker at the crease of the fold. Repeat with the other end of the curve. You have now placed three markers and divided the curve into four equal sections. Repeat the process until there are about 2 in. between each marker. Divide the number of stitches that you are picking up by the number of spaces in which to pick them up (the number of markers you've placed plus 1) to determine how many stitches to pick up between each marker. Feel free to improvise a little to keep the curve even, as long as the result is the total number asked for by the pattern.

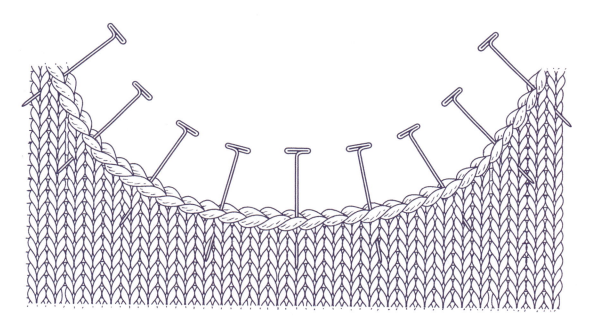

To pick up stitches evenly on a curve, divide the curve into equal sections, then pick up equal numbers of stitches in each section.

3

Good Knitting Gone Wrong

You've adopted good knitting habits and you know your way around a knitting pattern like a pro. So you've knitting emergency-proofed yourself, right?

Unfortunately not. The plain truth is that no matter how long you've been knitting, mistakes happen. Our good news is that, with few exceptions, every knitting problem has a solution.

Tool Trouble

What happens if I don't have (lost, left somewhere else) the other needle for my project and I need to knit?

We hope you have one other needle of the same size (diameter) in your bag, even if it's made of another material, not the same length, or currently has another project on it. If there is knitting on it, you can transfer that project to a stitch holder or a piece of yarn or a smaller set of needles and then use the just-freed needle for your current project. You can also knit back and forth on a circular needle or from one single-pointed needle to several double-pointed needles used in a row to hold lots of stitches. Let your imagination run wild. As long as you have two needles of the same size, you can work it out.

In a pinch, you can even knit with two needles of different diameters (as long as one is the correct size). If you can find another needle that's just a size or two smaller, you can use it for a while because one of the best kept secrets in knitting is that it is the shaft of the right needle that governs the size of the stitch. You can lurch along with two needles of different sizes if you are willing to switch your stitches from needle to needle so that you are always knitting the stitches onto a needle of the correct size.

If you're needle-less and desperate, look around you. Have you ever tried knitting on pencils or chopsticks? Nepalese women straighten out wire hangers and use them to knit with. People from Peru knit on bicycle spokes. Necessity is the mother of knitting invention.

If you find yourself misplacing one of your needles with alarming frequency, you might want to seriously consider changing over to a circular needle.

When You Absolutely, Positively Need to Knit

Marion and Ahza were teaching an after-school knitting class at a YMCA. The children ranged in age from 5 to 11 years. The Y provided all the materials, including the needles, but the children were not allowed to take their needles home. When they arrived for one of the classes, one student ran to Ahza with great excitement, saying, "Look what I did at home!" She was holding up the beginnings of a charming scarf. Her stitches, however, were not on knitting needles (because they could not be taken home) but on ballpoint pens that she had cleverly discovered could be used as substitutes.

EMERGENCY TOOL SUBSTITUTIONS

TOOL	Substitute
This book	There is no substitute.
Tape measure	Standard sheet of paper: Paper measures 8½ in. wide by 11 in. long; with creative folding you can use it for measuring.
Scissors	Nail clippers. Teeth: In a dire emergency, you can try to bite through your yarn.
Stitch markers	Contrasting yarn: Use short pieces of a yarn that contrasts with your knitting yarn; tie the pieces around your needle where you need them.
Stitch holders	Contrasting yarn: Thread a tapestry needle with contrasting yarn and slide the stitches onto the yarn from the knitting needle; remember to tie the ends of the contrasting yarn together. No tapestry needle? Work the yarn through the stitches with the other knitting needle or a crochet hook.
Safety pins and straight pins	Paper clips: Straighten them out, then bend them again according to your need. Don't push them into the strand of yarn as you place them. (This substitution is not recommended if you are pinning something for blocking.)
Row counter	Paper and a pen or pencil: Make sure you make a hash mark as soon as you come to the end of the row; otherwise, several stitches into the next row you'll wonder if you marked down the last row. Safety pins: Mark a row by pinning around one of the stitches, adding a safety pin every 5 or 10 rows.
Point protectors	Bottle cork: Stick the points into it. Rubber bands: Wind around the back or front ends of the needles.
Tapestry needle	Crochet hook: Use it to pull the working yarn through a stitch or to hide the ends of yarn and weave a seam. (Don't do this unless you're desperate; it's very tedious and difficult to keep the tension even.)
Crochet hook	Knitting needle: Can do anything that a crochet hook can, you just won't have that comforting hook to hold the yarn before it is pulled.
Cable needle	Smaller-size double-pointed needle: Should be large enough to hold the stitches. Bent paper clip or other cylindrical object: a straw or toothpick, anyone?

How do I stop my stitches from coming off my needles when I put my knitting down?

If you're knitting in the round, push the knitting onto the cable and use point protectors or bind the two ends of the needle together with a rubber band. If you're using single-pointed needles, push your knitting back to the knob end of the needle and use point protectors or substitutes listed in Emergency Tool Substitutions at left.

What do I do if my single-pointed needles aren't long enough to hold all my stitches?

You can always buy longer single-pointed needles, but most knitters use a circular needle instead. The advantages are that you can hold many more stitches on the cable than you can on a straight needle and it's more ergonomic because the weight of the knitting is always equally distributed between your hands. All this switch requires is getting used to a new idea. Think of a circular needle as two single-pointed ones that *weren't* separated at birth. The ends of the needles are attached to each other by a flexible cord, but they're still the same two needle points.

Make the switch from straight to circular this way. First, put away the empty straight needle so you won't get confused. Then insert one point of the circular needle into the first stitch of the next row (now on the remaining straight needle) and knit the rest of the row. At the end of the row, all the stitches should be on the circular needle so you can now put away the second straight needle. Turn the work around, pick up the other end of the circular needle, and use its point to work back across the row you just finished. At the end of the row, put the finished work in your left hand, pick up the other point in your right hand, and knit back across the row. Repeat ad infinitum.

How do I knit in the round?

When you knit in the round on one or more circular needles, you are always working on the same side of the garment in an ever-lengthening spiral. Of course, this will affect the look of the stitches. If the pattern directions call for stockinette, you would knit every round, so the bumps always will be on the inside of what you're knitting. If you want to knit in garter stitch, you will need to alternate a knit round and a purl round to make the purl bumps appear on the side of the fabric that's facing you on every other row. To convert a pattern written in rows to knitting in the round, just reverse the way the stitches are made every other row in the chart or instructions. Knit stitches become purl stitches, and purls become knits. To convert a pattern written in the round to knitting back and forth in rows, do the same thing, in reverse.

I'm knitting a hat on a circular needle and I've started the top decreases. I've now got so few stitches on my needle that I can't knit around anymore. What should I do?

When the length of the circular needle is greater than the diameter of the knitting, find (or purchase) another circular needle of the same size (diameter). The length isn't important. Knit half the stitches from your original needle (we'll call it Needle 1) with the new circular needle (Needle 2, see p. 60).

Push the stitches you've just knit on Needle 2 onto its connecting cable and let both points hang down behind Needle 1. We'll tell you when you need to use Needle 2 again.

Turn the work counterclockwise so that Needle 1 is facing you. The working yarn should be hanging from the last stitch on the right side of the stitches that are on the connecting cable of Needle 2.

Pick up the point of Needle 1 that is on the left, swing it across the front of the stitches on Needle 1, and begin to knit the stitches from

Knitting with Two Circular Needles

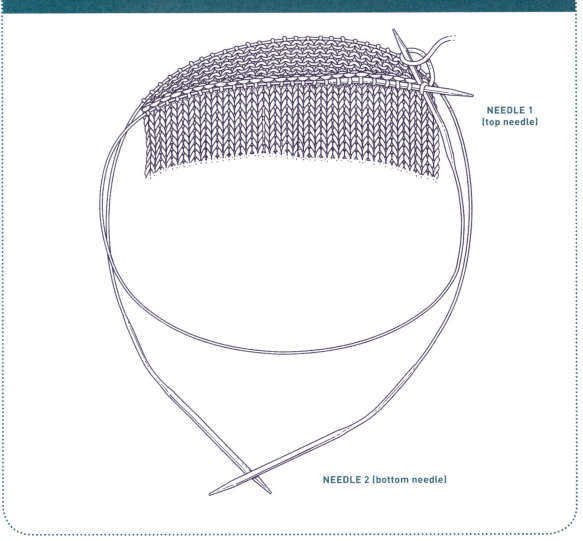

NEEDLE 1
(top needle)

NEEDLE 2 (bottom needle)

the other point of Needle 1 as if you were knitting across a row. When you finish knitting all the stitches on Needle 1, slide them to its connecting cable, let both points hang free, and turn your work so that Needle 2 is facing you.

Push the stitches up to the point of the right end of Needle 2 and use the other end of Needle 2 to knit them off. You're still knitting in the round, but each half of the round is knit on its own needle while the other needle hangs in the back of your work.

What if my circular needle is coiled up tight like a snake?

This often happens when you first take a circular needle out of its packaging. Circular needles relax their cables over time, but most of us don't want to wait that long.

If you have a hair dryer and a friend, ask your friend to hold the points of the needles so that the connecting cable is stretched out to its full length. Blow back and forth on the connecting plastic with your hair dryer set to medium until the cable straightens out. If you are friendless (we suggest you join a knitting circle) or don't own a hair dryer, place the needle in hot water, let it sit for a while, and it should relax some.

In both cases, once you're done, hang the needle up by one end and let the weight of the other end relax the cable even more. One way to do this is to use a clothespin to attach one point to a hanger, and leave the needle to dangle overnight. If it doesn't uncoil enough to suit you, repeat the whole process.

It's not a good idea to store a circular needle in the original package, as it tends to coil up again in a confined space. We store ours in resealable plastic food storage bags (1-qt. capacity) and write the U.S. and metric needle numbers on the outside. To keep all of them together, punch a hole in one corner of each bag and put them in order of size on a metal ring that opens, or tie the bags together with a ribbon or piece of yarn.

What do I do if I'm making a poncho and I can't fit all the stitches onto my circular needle anymore?

When your circular needle is too short to hold all your stitches, look for another circular needle of the same size. If you have one, using it will save you from having to stop your work until you can buy another circular needle of a longer length that you may never need again.

Knit a portion of the stitches (how many is governed by the relative lengths of the two circular needles) onto the new needle and finish the round by knitting the rest of the stitches onto the original needle with its other point. Continue, knitting each set of stitches back onto its own needle, as described on p. 59.

What do I do if I'm making a shawl and I'm running out of room on my circular needle?

If you are knitting back and forth on a circular needle and you now have too many stitches

Be Sure You Knit with the Correct Needle Point

When knitting with two circular needles, it's vital to make sure you are always knitting with the other end of the needle that is holding the stitches you're about to knit. We tug on the end of the point we're planning to knit with and, if we don't feel the tug on the needle that is holding the stitches, we know we're holding the point of the wrong needle and we try again with another point.

to fit on it, the solution is the same as for the poncho, except that you'll turn around and knit back at the end of the row. You can add more circular needles if you have to. You might use several circulars if you're knitting rounds around the outside of an afghan or rug.

I knit with the wrong point and all of my stitches are on one needle! What do I do now?
Everyone who has used two circular needles in this way has done this at some time or another. Slip the stitches that you've just knit onto the other needle. The very worst that can happen is that you have to take out the stitches you have knit up and start again using the correct end of the correct needle.

I'm knitting on double-pointed needles and all these needle points are making me crazy! Is there an easier way?
It's very common to feel as if there were so many needles that there's no room for fingers. All the needles stick out in different directions, threatening to poke you in the tender parts of your anatomy. You'll feel more in control if you keep the needles you're working with on top of the others and try to forget the others' existence until you need them. Don't worry, the needles you're not using will settle down after you've knit the first inch or so and you'll hardly notice them.

How do I stop my socks from having ladders in them where I changed from one needle to the next?
When working with double-pointed needles or two circular ones, knit the first stitch on each needle, pull the working yarn taut, and knit the second stitch as tightly as you can. If this doesn't correct the problem, knit the first two stitches of the next needle onto the previous one. Place a stitch marker to mark the beginning of the round, as you'll be moving the stitches around the needles.

What happens if I drop a stitch marker?
It's our opinion that some manufacturers make their markers out of jumping beans, ready to leap off your needle at the slightest provocation. Lay your needles down carefully and find the marker or get another one.

If you've knit beyond the point where the marker fell off, the markers that remain on the needle can tell you where to place the marker that escaped. If your markers are for pattern repeats, count the stitches between the two markers surrounding the missing one and set it back on your needle in the correct place.

If you've placed markers to ensure consistent shaping, when knitting a raglan sweater, for example, count the stitches on the other side of the garment and replace your marker to match.

If it's an end-of-round marker, look for the cast-on tail. Depending on the kind of cast on you used, the tail comes out of the first stitch you cast on or the last. Frankly, if you're off by a stitch, it's not the end of the world. Follow the stitch up until you reach your needle and place your marker.

Yarn Emergencies

How do I find the end of the yarn that's inside the ball?
Some yarn manufacturers wind their balls so it's almost impossible to find the inside end. However, the secret is to dig around with your fingers until you find a clump of yarn that seems to be in the center and pull it out. If you're lucky, the clump will come out with only one strand going back into the ball. Unravel the clump and wind it around the ball until you come to the end. If the clump comes out without a visible end, put your fingers back in the ball and pull out another clump. You can also try to determine which strand is leading to the end and which goes to the rest of the ball.

I'm getting to the end of my first ball of yarn; should I tie the end of this ball to the beginning of the next?

Never join any two balls of yarn with a knot! A knot can come undone and it's horrifying to see a hole developing in the middle of your chest (or bosom) as the two strands of yarn that you thought you firmly knotted together pull out through the stitches on either side. Also, **no knots** is a matter of principle for Marion and Ahza. Join your new ball our way:

1. Leave a 6-in. tail of the yarn you've been knitting with so that you'll have enough to weave in during the finishing process. If necessary, unknit some of the stitches to get it.

2. Insert your right needle into the next stitch on the left needle as if you were going to work it.

3. Loop the new yarn over the right needle leaving a 6-in. tail (Figure 1).

4. Holding onto both strands of the new yarn, complete the stitch, drawing the new yarn through the old stitch and slipping the old stitch off the needle.

5. When you've completed 4 or 5 sts, you may want to go back and tie (without knotting) the tails of the old and new yarn together to secure them temporarily.

I don't have quite enough yarn to finish the row. Can I join a new ball midrow?

The answer is, it depends. If you're making a project whose edges will show (like a scarf), we actually recommend that you join a new ball in the middle of a row.

If you're knitting a piece that will be joined to another (for example, the front piece of a pullover, which will be joined to the back piece), it's a good idea to join at the end of a row

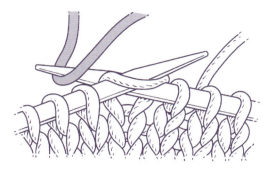

FIGURE 1
Loop the new yarn over the right needle.

because, if you can't use the ends to join the seam, at least you can hide them in the seam.

If you are knitting in the round, join the new ball in a place where it won't be seen (meaning, not in the center of the front of your sweater).

I've run out of yarn and my project isn't finished! What do I do now?

Even if you buy extra balls of yarn, changes in gauge, in the pattern, or—heaven forbid—a

 We Want to Warn You

Never try to knit directly from a skein. Although this seems like a timesaver, it is a recipe for disaster because, as you knit, the skein degenerates into a tangled clump. The only solution is to find the other end and start winding it into a ball, threading it through the tangles.

How to Wind the Perfect Ball of Yarn

Arrange your skein of yarn over the back of a chair or over a friend's hands so it stays in a circle. Find one end and hold it against your left palm, leaving a 6-in. tail. Bring the end behind your thumb and wind the yarn around your thumb and index finger in the shape of a figure 8 (Figure 1). Continue winding until you have at least 10 loops. Place your right thumb and index finger over the place where the yarn crosses (Figure 2) and pull the yarn off your left hand. Fold the group of loops in half and put it back in your left hand with the loose tail hanging over the thumb from front to back (Figure 3). Wind the yarn from the skein around the loops.

When you feel there are enough loops in one direction, shift the ball between your fingers and begin winding in a new place, making sure the tail is kept free. Always place some of your fingers between the ball and the yarn you're wrapping around it so that you don't wind the yarn too tightly (Figure 4). When you are finished, you will be able to pull the yarn from either end.

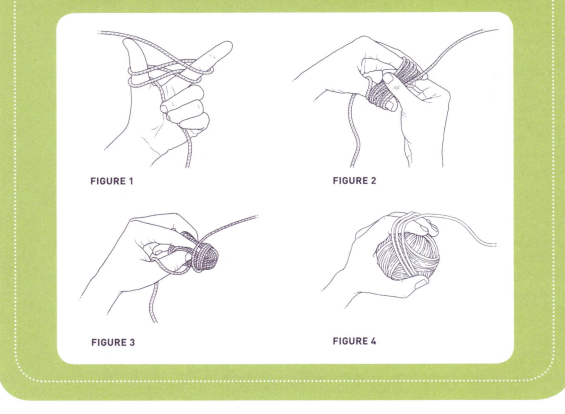

FIGURE 1

FIGURE 2

FIGURE 3

FIGURE 4

typo can cause you to come up short. Grab the label from the yarn and immediately call the shop where you bought it. If you're lucky, they will still have some balls of the same dye lot in stock. If they don't, check other yarn stores in the area and, if that doesn't yield more yarn, try the Internet or the yarn manufacturer.

You can also search for your yarn on www .ravelry.com. Unfortunately, they don't include dye lot information so you'd have to request that information by email before you buy.

However, if you've been working on this project for a long time, there may be no more yarn to be had of the same dye lot, color, or even brand. Don't despair.

- It is sometimes possible to work in yarn of the same color but a different dye lot by alternating the old ball with the new ball every round or every two rows for a couple of inches before you keep knitting with the new dye lot alone. As a last resort, you can unravel your work back to the beginning and alternate the balls from the start.

- If you have to use another color, look at the pattern and see where you might sensibly work it in. The amount of yarn you're short will help you choose the best solution. You might want to knit all the edgings and pockets in the new color. You could consider striping the garment or making the sleeves in the new color.

- If you have to use a yarn from a different manufacturer, make sure that the gauges are the same and the yarns look good together when they are knit up. Also, make sure that the washing instructions are the same for both fibers.

How do I stop the yarn from twisting between my knitting and the ball?

Part of the process of making most yarns is twisting the individual fibers together to give the yarn strength. Much of the time it doesn't matter if you knit with or against the twist. But if your yarn is twisting back on itself, that does matter; it means that you are knitting against the twist, untwisting the yarn a bit with each stitch you make. The solution is to knit from the other end of the ball because you'll then be knitting with the twist.

If you can't get to the other end of the yarn, stand up, hold the ball of yarn in one hand, and let your knitting dangle. It should untwist and you'll be untwisted for a bit before you have to repeat the process.

Marion, Rebel Joiner

She hasn't admitted this to Ahza but, sometimes, when joining a new yarn, Marion knits the next stitch with both the old and the new strand of yarn. On the next row she makes sure to knit the two strands as one stitch. It feels like a firmer temporary join than tying a bow. This doesn't always work, especially with thicker yarns, so a trial run comes first.

If you want to try this, too, no one need know but yourself.

Better Safe Than Sorry: How to Avoid Running Out of Yarn

If you're making something like an afghan or scarf, it's possible to figure out how much yarn you're going to need fairly soon after you've started knitting. For example, if you want to make an 8-ft.-long scarf and have bought eight balls of yarn to do it, measure how long the scarf is after knitting one ball. If it's less than 12 in., you won't have enough yarn. At that point, you can trot yourself back to the yarn store to buy what you need or, if that's not an option, content yourself with a shorter or narrower scarf.

Determining whether you have enough yarn for a sweater is a little trickier. If your pattern has a schematic, you can figure out the total number of square inches in the project, knit the first ball of yarn, measure the square inches it produces, and see how the two compare. If you don't have a schematic or you're not in the mood for mathematics, then knit up the front or back and a sleeve and see how much yarn you have left. If it's less than half, you're in trouble. If it's exactly half, you're still going to be short, as you're likely going to need yarn to finish the neck. If you're knitting a sweater with long sleeves, and you've used up more than one fourth of your supply after completing the front or back, you're also in trouble because sleeves, especially if they are longer than the body of the sweater or quite wide, can use as much yarn as a front or back. However you approach this, the goal is to find out as early as possible whether you need more yarn so you can locate it from the same dye lot.

Knitting Emergencies

I put my knitting down midway through a row/round; how do I know in which direction to knit?

In midrow, the yarn that you're knitting with should always be hanging from the last stitch on the right needle. If it isn't, you're about to knit in the wrong direction. Turn your knitting around.

If you've picked up stitches that have flown off your needle when you weren't looking, the working yarn may now be in the middle of the needle. Slip the stitches from one needle to the other until the working yarn is hanging from the last stitch on the right needle. Then, *unknit* this stitch. If the working yarn moves back to the previous stitch on the right needle, you're knitting in the correct direction. However, if the working yarn moves over to the left needle, turn the knitting around before you continue.

To keep this from happening in the future, always knit to the end of a row or round before stopping.

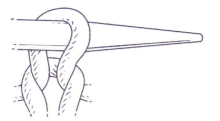

CORRECT

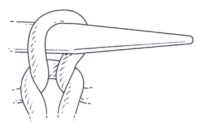

INCORRECT

In almost all cases, the front leg of the stitch should be slightly closer to the point of the left needle.

Some of my stitches look funny, sort of twisted. What happened?

Okay, here comes the lecture on *stitch mount*. Pick up your knitting and look at the first stitch on the left needle. The parts of the stitch that hang over the needle are called the legs. The way the legs are positioned on the needle is called the stitch mount. Although there are some exceptions (usually determined by where in the world you learned to knit), the leg in front of the needle should always be slightly closer to the point of the left needle. If you accidentally work a stitch through the back leg, the result is a twisted stitch.

When the stitch is mounted incorrectly, there are three ways to fix it. One is to slip the stitch to the right needle and turn it as you slip it back to the left needle. The second, more daring, approach is to let the stitch slide off the needle and to turn it around with your fingers before putting it back on the needle. Last, you can either knit or purl (whatever your pattern says)

into the back leg of the twisted stitch and it will turn itself around. Don't, however, try this if you're knitting a complicated stitch pattern; take it out and reknit.

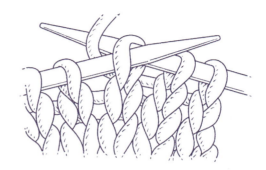

Knitting into the back of a twisted stitch to correct the stitch mount

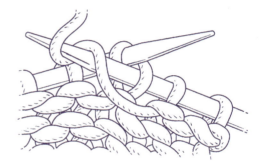

Purling into the back of a twisted stitch to correct the stitch mount

I've completely lost track of which row I'm knitting. How do I get started again?

The ounce of prevention: It is false pride to think that you will remember the number of the row you're currently knitting. That's what row counters are for. We use row counters that slip over or hang from the needle so they cannot be ignored before you knit the next row.

Because you haven't done that, look at the pattern and find the first row of the part of the pattern you're currently working. Then look at your knitting and identify the matching row. This should be fairly easy because new row counts usually begin at a change, such as rows that contain increases or decreases, a color change, or a change in the number of stitches. Put a small safety pin around one stitch of this row to mark it as row 1. Then count each row above row 1 and put another safety pin in row 5 and then row 10 and so on until you get to the loops on your needle. This is the number of the row you are on. *Write it down!*

If you don't have any safety pins, thread a tapestry needle with a long piece of yarn of a contrasting color. Weave it between two stitches on row 1, and pull it through to the other side, leaving a short tail. Count up to the 5th row and bring the contrasting yarn forward between two stitches on that row. Continue as instructed above.

My scarf is becoming a tube. What's going on?

Are you using stockinette stitch? If so, the stitches pull in one direction and will cause the sides of your fabric to curl toward each other. To lessen the curl, start and end each row with 3 sts in seed stitch (Row 1: K1, p1, k1, work in stockinette to the last 3 sts, k1, p1 k1. Repeat for all rows.). You can also try using a needle two or three sizes larger because if the stitches are loose, they pull less. However, these fixes may not solve the problem. If you alternate knit and purl stitches in the same row (as in rib stitch or seed stitch), or knit every row, or create horizontal stripes in different stitch patterns, you'll end up with a flatter, if not flat, scarf.

The edges of my shawl look so bumpy. What am I doing wrong?

Nothing. If you're beginning or ending the row in garter stitch, these bumps are to be expected. If you are using stockinette stitch at the beginning and end of a row, knit the first and last stitches through the back loop on the knit side and purl the first and last stitches on the purl side by bringing the yarn under rather than over the needle to make most of the bumps disappear.

All bumpy side edges can be transformed into straight ones by adding one stitch to each end of the cast-on row (these are called selvedge stitches). For example: Cast on 44 sts rather than the 42 sts your pattern calls for. Slip the first stitch in each row as if to knit, and knit the last stitch. The result will be one side stitch that looks like a V over every two rows.

If you can't or don't want to add stitches, the edges will look less bumpy if you pull on the first stitch in every row after you work it.

Ohmygawd, I've dropped a stitch. Can you help me?

Don't move (especially your knitting), take three deep breaths, and try to relax. Now, look down at your knitting calmly. What you need to do, as soon as possible, before it has a chance to unravel any farther, is secure the dropped stitch by catching it on a safety pin and closing the pin. Once you do that, it can't go anywhere. With your stitch secured, consider

A Useful Digression on Selvedge

Use selvedge stitches when you know that you will be joining two pieces side to side that will have alternating stitch patterns—for example, several rows in garter stitch followed by several rows of stockinette. Add 1 st to each side and knit them on every row.

the situation. How far down is the lost stitch from your needle? If it's just a row or two back, you've got two options:

1. Unknit

You can unknit your stitches back to the dropped stitch, pop it back on the needle, and proceed from there. Unknitting is the safest way to take out your knitting. With needles and knitting in hand, look at the last stitch on the right needle (the first one that you want to take out). It has the piece of yarn that you're using to knit with (the working yarn) hanging out of a loop located just below the loop over the needle. If you can't see where the working yarn has gone, tug gently on it to identify the loop it's coming through.

Insert the point of the left needle through this loop from front to back (Figure 1) so the stitch

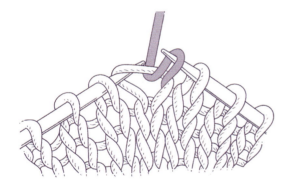

FIGURE 1

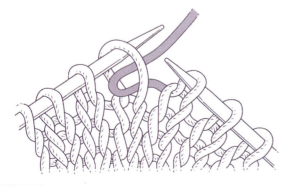

FIGURE 2

mount will be correct (see p. 67 for an explanation of stitch mount); then slide the loop onto the left needle. Release the loop on the right needle. Tug gently on the working yarn, and it will slide out of the loop (Figure 2). Continue in the same way, stitch by stitch, with the stitches leaving the right needle and going onto the left needle. At the end of the row, turn your knitting so that the needle full of stitches is in your right hand and continue. Congratulations! You're unknitting.

This method is great for anxious knitters because it makes it almost impossible to drop a stitch. It's also good to use when you're taking out less than a row, and it's often necessary in lace knitting. But, as you will soon find out, it's slow and gets old pretty quickly if you've got a lot to take out.

A slightly more dangerous but faster way to unknit is to slide several stitches off the right needle at one time. Hold the stitches under their loops with your fingers and, as you pull the yarn through each stitch, place it back on the left needle, making sure that the stitch mount is correct. As your confidence increases, you'll find you can take out quite a number of stitches at a time this way.

To unknit, the first step is to insert the left needle into the stitch *below* the one you want to unknit, as is shown here. You will then pull the right needle back just a bit, as indicated by the arrow, to release the stitch.

Here the stitch has been released from the right needle, allowing the working yarn to be pulled out.

2. Knit it back up

You can "knit" the dropped stitch back up using a crochet hook. (You can also do this with an extra knitting needle, but it can be awkward to work with.)

⬤ Know Your Stitch Count

It is of paramount importance to know that you're working with the correct number of stitches so you know as soon as possible if you've dropped a stitch or mistakenly picked up extras. That's why we tell beginning knitters to count their stitches at the end of every few rows to make sure they're still on count. To make double sure, always count your stitches as many times as it takes to come up with the same number twice. It's not difficult to count 2 sts as one or to think that a stitch with split threads is two stitches instead of one. Counting your stitches at least twice will lessen the possibility of that happening.

Another way to keep yourself on stitch count is to use stitch markers. While casting on, if you place a stitch marker after every 20 sts (or any other multiple that suits you), you'll never have to count again after you've counted those cast-on stitches twice. Markers can also be used to set off shaping stitches or to delineate pattern repeats and are an essential aid for keeping your place in a chart. If you are knitting a lace pattern, put a stitch marker after each pattern repeat and always count your stitches after each row so you can catch mistakes right away. Otherwise you're setting yourself up for lots of unknitting.

In stockinette or reverse stockinette

If you're on the knit side (the stitches look like Vs), transfer the dropped stitch onto the crochet hook with the hook facing up. You should see a horizontal bar of yarn between the two stitches above the dropped stitch. Catch this bar with the crochet hook, turn your hook downward, and pull this bar through the dropped stitch. Carefully ease the resulting loop off the hook, grasping it between your thumb and index finger. Turn the stitch around so that the stitch mount is correct and put it back on the crochet hook. Repeat this process until there are no more bars above the stitch, then transfer this stitch back to your left needle. Make sure you place the stitch on the needle so the stitch mount is correct.

If you are on the purl side of stockinette stitch (bumps on every row), just turn your work around so the knit side is facing you and follow the instructions just given.

In garter stitch

Garter stitch consists of all knit rows, which means that on both sides of your knitting you're going to have to contend with both Vs (the front of the knit stitch) and bumps (the back of the knit stitch, or a purl). No problem. If you have dropped a stitch more than a row back, turn your work until you're positioned to pick up the first stitch on the knit side of the row, work it up, and turn your work around to work up the

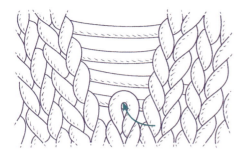

Insert your crochet hook into the dropped stitch where indicated, front to back.

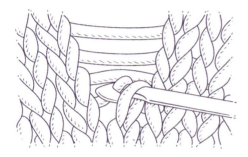

With the hook facing down, grab the bar behind the dropped stitch and pull it through. Continue as needed.

next stitch (which is now a knit stitch). As you continue toward the top of your work, you'll always be picking up the stitch from the knit side and turning your work to make it so.

Sometimes the dropped stitch is so many rows back that the stitches on either side of it have come together and there's not enough slack yarn between them to knit the stitch back up or, if you did, you would see the effect of the pulling in your finished project. Once again, you've got two options:

1. Live with it

Leave the dropped stitch on the safety pin to deal with when you finish your garment (see p. 84). You'll need to compensate for the dropped stitch so increase a stitch in the next row on the public side.

2. Rip it

If you're knitting a complicated pattern that's now been thrown off because of the dropped stitch, or you can't bear the thought of this imperfection in your knitting (be honest with yourself about this—better to admit now you won't be able to live with it than when you've finished the piece), you must rip.

Ripping (or frogging, as it's also known—*rip it! rip it!*) requires taking your knitting off the needles and pulling the knitting out until you reach your mistake. For many knitters, the mere notion of ripping out their work gives them heart palpitations. But there is no need to panic if you use our tried-and-true four-step method.

FIGURE 1

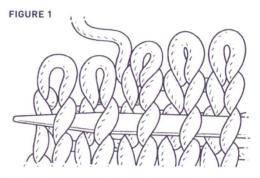

Threading your needle through a row of knit stitches before ripping.

FIGURE 2

Threading your needle through a row of purl stitches before ripping.

1. Mark your mistake by putting a pin in or around it.

2. Weave a needle into the row below the mistake. If it's a row with Vs facing you, put your needle under the right side and over the left side of each V (Figure 1 on p. 71). Purl stitches are handled in the same way, except that the Vs are concealed between the bumps (Figure 2 on p. 71).

3. Remove your other needle from your knitting. Pull out the stitches until you reach the needle you inserted. Your stitches are back on the needle as if by magic.

4. As you work the next row, check to make sure that your stitches are mounted correctly.

Why is my scarf getting narrower and narrower?

Could it be that you have fewer stitches on your needle than when you cast on? The sooner you realize this, the better. The first thing to do is to figure out why you don't have enough stitches.

- **Did you drop any of them?**
  Always check for this first, because an unsecured dropped stitch can unravel right back to the cast-on row.

- **Did you forget to do a yarn over?**
  If you discover you've made this omission on the row after you should have made your yarn over, you don't need to unknit back to the scene of the crime, though you can if you want to. Instead, pull up the thread between the stitches where the yarn over should have been and knit into it.

The Most Original Hat on the Isle of Manhattan

Actually, there's a third option—besides unknitting and using a crochet hook—when you've dropped a stitch.

While teaching a "Learn to Knit with Your Child" class, Ahza had a very young student who dropped stitches. No matter how hard she tried to concentrate, she would drop a stitch every 2 or 3 in. As a result, the student was becoming frustrated and less enthusiastic about knitting. Ahza asked her to put a safety pin in each dropped stitch and showed her a simple increase so the number of stitches on her needle would remain the same. Confronted with a finished hat with a multitude of safety pins, Ahza had the girl thread different colors of yarn through each loop and tie them in bows. She now has the most unusual hat in her school and everyone wants one just like it.

Moral: If you make a mistake once, it's a mistake. If you make a mistake more than once, it's a design element.

• Did you forget to knit into a yarn over?
Maybe you didn't knit into a yarn over from the row before (the equivalent of a dropped stitch) or you knitted an intended yarn over with the next stitch.

The no-fail solution for a lost stitch is to go back to it by unknitting or ripping and then to be sure to pick up or make the stitch. But if it's a straightforward pattern, with no intricate color work or stitch patterns, you can simply add stitches to make up for the ones you've lost (assuming you've established without a doubt that you don't have a dropped stitch hanging out somewhere). Knit into the front and back of stitches chosen for their unobtrusiveness, spreading the extra stitches over several rows if you're short several stitches, until you've got the correct number again. Our lips are sealed.

Why is the back of my sweater getting wider and wider?
You may be adding stitches (inadvertently, of course). The most common causes of extra stitches are the following:

- Knitting into the underside of the first stitch. The underside of the first stitch of a row has two loops. If you knit into both of these loops, you'll add a stitch. You can avoid this by pulling the working yarn under the needle and to the back before you knit the first stitch of a row. If the first stitch is a purl, make sure that the yarn is hanging straight down. This mistake is easy to find because it's on the edge of whatever you're making (see p. 74).

- Bringing the yarn into position to work the next stitch and then absentmindedly slipping the stitch from the left needle to the right needle without working it. This will result in not only an extra loop on your needle but also an unknitted stitch. If this is what you've done, you'll see a bar and a hole next to it. Treat the unworked stitch like a dropped one (see p. 68), pulling the bar through the unknit stitch.

- Forgetting to bring the yarn *between* the needles when you switch from a knit stitch to a purl. This causes an unintentional yarn over and, if you knit into it on the next row, there will be a hole underneath it.

- Picking up an unintended yarn over on a previous row and knitting into it. A hole will appear under the yarn over.

- Splitting a stitch when you knitted it and bringing up a piece of the stitch below. If you knit into both of these, you won't have a hole, but your fabric won't look quite right.

Done to excess, extra stitches will lead to a piece that is wider than it should be and/or develops unintended ruffles. Extra stitches also wreak havoc on stitch patterns. To fix the fabric, you'll either have to unknit (see p. 69) or rip down (see p. 71) to remove the added stitch or stitches.

However, if you're not a perfectionist and it's not essential to have the correct number of stitches on each row or between each marker on every row, there is an easier way to fix this. You can knit each extra stitch together with a stitch next to it in the following row. If you've knitted well beyond the point where you first picked up the stitch(es) and if it doesn't interfere with your pattern, simply knit pairs of stitches together (spacing them over a row or round if you've added more than 1 st) to get back to the right stitch count. If you do this carefully, it won't be obvious.

Why does my knitting seem to be changing size when my stitch count hasn't changed?

The size of your knitting, whether smaller or larger, is caused by a change in gauge. Although we know you went to great pains to ensure that you achieved gauge before you began this project, it's quite common for gauge to change after you've been knitting for a while. For instance, your mood can change your tension, causing you to knit either more loosely or more tightly.

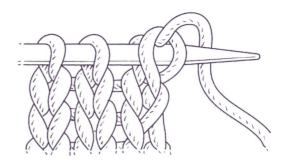

One way stitches get added is mistaking one stitch for two. In this example, it looks as if the needle has 4 stitches on it. There are only 3. The first 2 "stitches" are really the underside of the first stitch.

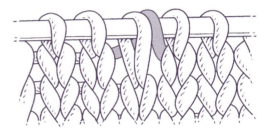

An extra stitch added by mistakenly slipping a stitch from the left to the right needle without knitting it.

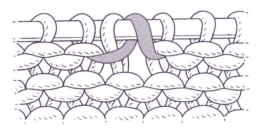

An extra stitch added by mistakenly slipping a stitch from the left to the right needle without purling it.

The solution to gauge change is to change needle sizes. Measure and compare the gauge at the beginning of this piece with your current gauge. Make another gauge swatch and, following our instructions on p. 10, increase or decrease the size of your needles, until you achieve the original gauge again.

Ripping back to where your gauge started to change and reknitting with the new size needle is the solution for the perfectionist. But if you are knitting on needles smaller than size 8 and there is no more than a change of two needle sizes required to get back to gauge, it's possible that you can start knitting with the new size needles and let careful blocking (see p. 99) take care of the rest. To make the change of needle even less obvious, knit with one of each size for 1 in. or so before changing over entirely to the new size.

What have I done to my knitting?
You look at what you've been knitting and it looks wrong, even though your stitch count is correct. Perhaps your lovely diamond-shaped pattern has gone ragged or your lace has developed unexpected holes. Then you realize—you knit when you should have purled, purled when you should have knit. Or you forgot a yarn over.

The most drastic solution is to rip back to the first mistake and reknit, but you may want to try these less draconian fixes first. In all cases, you must first identify and then mark with a safety pin the place or places where you went wrong.

If you knit a stitch or stitches instead of purling them, or vice versa, deliberately drop the stitch or stitches back to the mistake (see "The Deliberate Drop" on p. 77), correct it, and work the stitch or stitches back up, making sure you are following the stitch pattern. It's important to keep your tension even when you do this, especially if there's more than one stitch involved.

What's happening to my ribbing?
You've probably knit where you should have purled or vice versa. Try the Deliberate Drop before you rip. So that this won't happen in the future, here's how to tell a knit from a purl. Look at a knit stitch: The side facing you looks

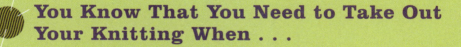

You Know That You Need to Take Out Your Knitting When . . .

- You've made a mistake that bothers you.
- Your knitting looks really wrong and you have no idea what you did or how to fix it.
- The mistake that you've made throws off the whole row or even the rest of your knitting.
- Your stitch count is off and the pattern you're knitting requires that it be accurate.
- Your gauge has changed noticeably.
- You've made a mistake that will make your project unusable. Mostly this is a mistake in shaping. Remember Flora (p. 45) whose sweater had a sleeve coming out of the front?

When You're Worried and You Can't Sleep, Count Your Stitches Instead of Sheep . . .

Marion got a call from Lily, who said that she needed some help with a tank top that didn't fit. Indeed, when she tried it on for Marion, it was a most peculiar object. It was very tight around the bust and the armholes came up to her chin. "But I followed the instructions exactly and my gauge is perfect." Lily said, "How could this happen to me? The instructions must be wrong."

Marion looked at the instructions and counted Lily's stitches. The number of stitches in each round of knitting varied, sometimes too many and sometimes too few. *Many* too few in the bust area. Then Marion counted the rows. The decreases all had too few rows between them. Lily had started the armholes with too few stitches on her needles and since she only *thought* she knew how to count rows, the armholes were much too short.

"We're going to have to take this out, probably down to waist level."

"But it's on number 3 needles!" Lily exclaimed.

Fortunately, this story has a happy ending—and a moral. When Lily returned for her next lesson, the tank top fit like a glove. The moral: Count your stitches and rows early and often.

like a V and, if you turn the stitch around, you can see a bump on the back. Look at a purl stitch: The bump is now in the front and the back of the stitch is a V. The difference between a knit and purl stitch is where the bump is. When you knit, the bump is in back; when you purl, it's in front.

Bump placement is responsible for the look of a stitch pattern. Take stockinette stitch, for example. By knitting one row and purling the next, you're placing all the Vs on one side and all the bumps on the other, making it smooth on one side, textured on the other.

What do I do if I skipped an armhole decrease?

Even though this sounds like a mistake that requires ripping, you can do the decrease row right now and compensate for it by knitting fewer rows before you decrease again. This solution will also work if you haven't worked an increase row in the right place or if you've skipped a single increase or decrease. Just remember that if the piece you are knitting is going to be attached to another one, you need to repeat your "variation" on the other piece so they will fit together correctly.

If I have to rip this sock/sweater/scarf out one more time, I'm going to throw it in the trash and never knit again. Can I be helped?

Maybe you don't have to rip. Although there are times when you must, there are many more times when you can leave the mistake in and knit on. Knitting is meant to be enjoyed, not to work your last nerve.

But before you knit on, consider whether or not you're the type of person who can live with a mistake. If you know that you will be bothered forever by being off by one stitch in a section of your lace shawl, unravel your knitting now, before you knit another stitch. If this isn't you, we want to reassure you that the Yarn Police are not going to take away your needles if you leave a mistake. After all, non-knitters can't see your mistakes and Real Knitters are too polite to mention them. In case we haven't convinced you and you'd like to be convinced, we give you full permission *not* to correct knitting mistakes if they don't affect the rest of your knitting. After all, craftspeople in many other cultures left mistakes in their hand work on purpose so their god or gods wouldn't be offended by their perfection. Let self-knowledge be your guide.

I put this project down five weeks (months, years) ago. I'd like to finish it, but how do I figure out where I am?

We applaud you. The first step is to take a trip down memory lane and see if you can remember why you stopped working on this project to begin with. Reread the pattern. If it was too difficult to knit before, will it be too difficult now? Or perhaps you simply didn't enjoy knitting it. Every knitter has some patterns that he or she never wants to knit. It would be better to remember that this is one of them rather than having to learn it all over again.

The Deliberate Drop

The Deliberate Drop is an alternative to ripping. If you see that you've knit rather than purled a stitch several rows below, mark it with a pin. Then determine which stitch on your needle is directly above the errant stitch, take that stitch off the needle, and deliberately drop it until you get to the pin. Take out the pin, correct the stitch, and knit it back up to your needle using the method explained on pp. 70–71.

You can also use the Deliberate Drop to rework several stitches in a row. However, make sure you know exactly what you're doing with each of these stitches as you knit them back up to the needle.

The Deliberate Drop won't work if you increased or decreased when you shouldn't have because undoing a decrease will result in pulling in the fabric because you don't have enough yarn on that row, and undoing an increase will cause you to end up with extra yarn.

Do you still have enough yarn to complete the project? If you don't, you can try to get more. If you can't, consider adjusting the pattern (shorter sleeves, perhaps) or redesigning it, adding different yarn (see p. 63 for more on this).

If it's a pattern with a close fit, compare your current measurements to those you were knitting from. If they don't match up, depending on where you were in the pattern, you may be able to increase or decrease its size by going to larger or smaller needles (see pp. 74–75), but if you're too far along, ripping it out and starting again may be called for. Remember to check your gauge again before starting. Also, if you now need a larger size, you may also require more yarn to complete the project.

There's another alternative that doesn't require you to rip or adjust and gives you great knitting karma—finish the project as is and give it to someone else.

Knitting Overcomes Bureaucracy, or Surviving the Department of Motor Vehicles

As told to us by Mona, a stylishly dressed woman wearing an exquisite knitted skirt at the Taos Wool Festival.

Mona had just finished the skirt, tried it on, and was feeling shy about wearing it in public. It had a lot of intricate shaping, including pleats, and was quite form fitting. As she contemplated her outfit and thought about the day ahead, she realized that she'd put off renewing her drivers' license, and it expired that day. She needed to get it done *right now* and rushed off to the DMV, dreading a process usually filled with lots of time-consuming bureaucratic details. *Go to that window! Now to the one over there!* And on and on.

After waiting in line, she finally arrived at the first window and was greeted with "Did you knit your skirt?" from the clerk, who continued, "It's so beautiful! Let me help you with your forms." And the clerk proceeded to take our friend's forms to all the appropriate windows, doing all the running around herself. The task was completed in record time.

Never was a trip to the Department of Motor Vehicles smoother and more pleasant. Once again, knitting saves the day!

4

Don't Let Finishing Finish You Off

Congratulations! Your knitting is off the needles and almost done! But, as you might guess, it's still possible for questions and emergencies to arise.

There are two schools of thought about this last phase of a project, known as *finishing*. One is that impeccable finishing is the most important part of knitting. The other promotes finishing any way you can as long as it doesn't come apart and it looks good.

Our philosophy falls in the middle. Finishing is a process, just like knitting, with its own gratifications and pitfalls, and doing it well takes practice and time. The more projects you finish, the better you'll become and the more you'll enjoy the process.

It's-Off-the-Needles-But-I'm-Not-Done-Yet Emergencies

I've got pieces of yarn hanging down from my finished knitting. Should I cut them off?
No, no, no! These ends of yarn, also called tails, will work their way to the front and stick out if you don't take the time to weave them in. Even worse, the beautiful sweater that has taken you six months to knit will unravel sooner or later. How you weave your tails in depends on the stitch you've been knitting.

Bumps on the private side (garter stitch and stockinette stitch)
Thread the tail onto a tapestry needle. Then look closely at one of your rows near the tail on the private side of your knitting. It consists of alternating upper and lower bumps.

Now, going in one direction, weave the tail through each bump, either all the top bumps or all the bottom bumps. You can bring the needle down into the bumps from the top or up through the bumps from the bottom. Just be consistent. Often you'll have to try it and see what looks best, especially if both sides of your work are going to be seen (a scarf, for instance). Weave the yarn along for about 2 in. (at least 8 sts in bulky yarns), then stretch

Six Rules on Weaving Tails

1. Never leave less than a 6-in. tail when starting a new ball of yarn.
2. Always change direction at least once when you weave in the tail.
3. Wait until you're sure your project is just the way you want it before you weave your tails in.
4. Don't weave in tails that are on a seam until after the seam is joined because you can use the tails to join pieces together and you can hide the ends in the seams so they won't show.
5. Don't leave lumps. Lumps happen when you weave in too many ends in the same area (like the side of a scarf). Try to plan the places where you join another piece of yarn to avoid this.
6. Don't weave in the tails of yarn used to join pieces until you're sure that whatever you've made fits!

Garter Stitch Fabric

Reverse Stockinette Fabric (the private side of stockinette)

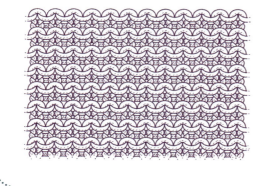

the knitting to make sure that the woven tail matches the tension of your work.

Now, turn your work around, move to another row of bumps, and weave back in the opposite direction for about 1 in., or half as much as you worked the other way. This will keep the yarn from coming loose.

Gently pull the knitting in all directions so that the tail has the same tension as the fabric. If you've knitted with very slippery yarn, you

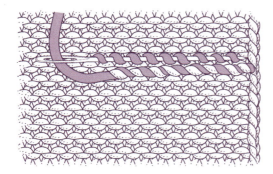

Weaving in a yarn end on the private side of a piece of stockinette

may want to turn around one more time, but in most cases one turn is enough.

Turn your work over to the public side. It should look the way it did before you started, and you should see little, if any, of the yarn woven into the back. If the woven tail shows through on the right side, decide how much this bothers you and consider pulling the tail out and starting again. Otherwise, leave it. If the fabric puckers, you need to adjust the tension of the tail.

Once you're happy, clip the extra yarn, leaving about ¼ in. so the yarn won't poke through to the right side. It will eventually sink out of sight.

Bumps on the public side (garter stitch and reverse stockinette)

The easy way to weave in yarn tails on the public side of the work is to do so just as you would if the bumps were on the private side. Then, after weaving, take the tail to the back of the work and clip it. Of course, that's not the *only* way.

The really invisible way of hiding the tail

Knitters of yore and purists of today use this method when stockinette stitch is involved—whether public or private side. But most people (including us) only use it when there is no other option. It's useful for making a repair on stockinette when you don't have access to the private side, or don't want to make even the smallest bumps (as when darning a sock), or when knitting a piece that is meant to be reversible.

The invisible way to weave in a tail on stockinette is to use *duplicate stitch*.

1. With the Vs facing (otherwise known as the knit side of stockinette), bring your tapestry needle up in the space just below where the two points of a V meet. Insert the needle horizontally through the bottom of the stitch directly above and pull the yarn through (Figure 1).

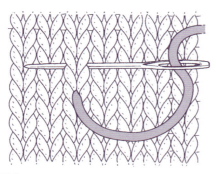

FIGURE 1

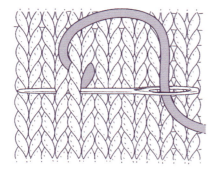

FIGURE 2

2. Go down into the first space that you came out of (Figure 2). You've just duplicated one stitch with your tail yarn and the needle. It should be lying happily and invisibly on top of the one you knitted.

3. Come up in the center of an adjacent V (Figure 3) and repeat the procedure. After you've duplicated 5 sts in this fashion, you can cut the yarn ¼ in. from the surface of the fabric on the private side. There's no need to change direction.

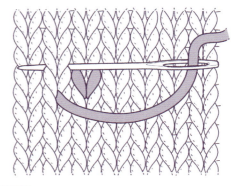

FIGURE 3

Ribbing and other textured stitches

It's very easy to hide the tail in ribbing. Just weave it through one leg of a vertical line of Vs (Figure 4) and come back in the opposite direction weaving through the other leg. For other textured stitches, experiment until you figure out what shows least.

I'm using bulky yarn and it's creating big bumps when I weave the ends. What should I do?

Divide the tail yarn into two parts and weave each in separately. Some knitters do this with all their tails. We don't.

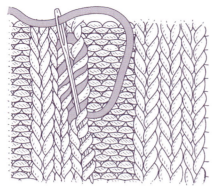

FIGURE 4
To hide a tail in ribbing, weave it through one leg of a vertical line of Vs, then come up in the opposite direction through the other leg.

I've got holes in my scarf—how do I fix them?
The only time that you *really* need to fix a hole is when it will grow larger in the future, and this usually involves a dropped stitch. Otherwise, let your knitting conscience be your guide.

Holes can happen when you change balls of yarn in the middle of a row (Figure 5). To make these disappear when you weave in the tails, first, undo any knots that you might have used

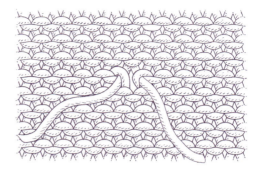

FIGURE 5
When you change balls of yarn in the middle of a row, you can end up with a small hole.

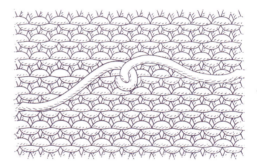

FIGURE 6
To get rid of it, wrap the yarn ends completely around one another (360 degrees), then weave them in.

Five Good Reasons to Learn the Duplicate Stitch

1. Perfectionists use it for weaving in all their tails.
2. You can use it to strengthen weak spots in the yarn.
3. You can use it in mending to fill a hole.
4. You can use it in color work, after you've finished the knitting, to correct mistakes or to put in a small patch or line of color. It is also used to make the one-stitch lines in argyle, which avoids having more strands hanging down than you absolutely need.
5. You can use it to make everyone think that you actually knitted the picture of the Mona Lisa into the front of your sweater.

to secure the two ends. Each tail will hang on either side of a small hole. Twist the tails completely around each other (360 degrees) until they are back where they started (Figure 6 on p. 83). It's especially important to wrap the yarns completely around each other if you're doing color work so you don't weave an end that is one color into knitting of a different color. We assure you that you'll be able to see it on the public side of your work if you do.

Now that you've covered up the hole, thread one end of the yarn into a needle and hide the tail using one of the methods described earlier. Thread the other piece and take another look on the public side of the piece to make sure the hole doesn't show. If it does, you can weave this piece of yarn behind the hole before you hide the tail.

Holes also appear when you are doing color knitting and forget to twist the yarns around each other when you change colors; they can also happen for reasons you can't quite figure out. The solution here is to thread a new piece of matching yarn, draw the edges of the hole together as best you can with it, then weave the ends in.

Hole-like spaces are caused by uneven stitches and loose tension. Figure out the path of the yarn in each of your giant stitches, then pull gently on the yarn in the adjacent stitches on the back of your piece. You may have to do this on several stitches before and after the monster stitch to even out the difference in tension and to shrink the hole.

If you actually have a hole (a rip) in your knitting, see p. 103.

What do I do with the dropped stitches on my scarf that I have hanging out on safety pins?
Because this situation involves live stitches, you have to fix it. Thread a tapestry needle with a 12-in. length of matching yarn, pull the yarn through the loop of the dropped stitch, remove the safety pin, and weave in the two ends.

Another option, if you have lots of dropped stitches on safety pins, is to leave the loops on the right side of the piece and replace the safety pins with buttons or beads or tie pieces of different colored yarn or ribbon around the dropped stitches. Thus you can turn your dropped stitches into a design element.

Now that my scarf is off the needles, it's curled into a tube—what should I do?
Many stitches, especially stockinette, pull the stitches out of alignment. This causes the edges of your knitting to curl under. Your best bet is to wet the scarf, pin it out straight, and let it dry completely. This process is called blocking; to learn more about it, see p. 99. We must warn you, though, that sometimes the curl will reappear, so don't let on to anyone that you didn't mean to make a tube scarf.

I know all these pieces are supposed be a sweater, but how do I put them together?
First, label each piece by pinning a piece of paper with its name to the public side. You want to be sure to be seaming the correct sides together, so you don't end up with a public side front and a private side back.

Most of the time, the pattern instructions will specify the order in which the pieces should be put together. If it doesn't, do what seems logical. This is how we would put a sweater together:

1. Join the shoulders.

2. Attach the sleeves to the body, starting and ending at the underarm.

3. Join side and sleeve seams. (Approach the armhole from the bottom of the side seam and from the cuff of the sleeve so the seams meet at the underarm.)

4. Finish the neck if necessary.

5. Do any necessary trim (buttonholes and pockets, for example).

How do I join the pieces of my sweater if they've curled into tubes?

If the pieces you are joining don't quite match in size or if they are curling at the edges, pin them out to the correct measurements on a flat surface. Put a thin cloth over the knitting and steam them with an iron. This will help resize and uncurl the pieces long enough to join them. *Warning:* Don't let your iron rest on the knitting. It might flatten the stitches or even stretch the pieces too much.

How do I join the front and back pieces of my sweater?

You're going to use a *side-to-side join*, which is what you also use to turn a piece of flat knitting into a tube (for example, joining the sides of sleeves together or the side edges of a hat). Side-to-side joins are always done on the public side and it's easiest to do them on a flat surface with the private sides facing down. Because we use invisible joins, exactly how you make a side-to-side join will depend on what stitch you used in your knitting.

To join two pieces worked in garter stitch side to side

With the edges of the two pieces placed together, public sides facing out, thread your needle through the bottom bump on the edge of one side and then through the top bump on the matching ridge on the other side. If you see that you're not going to come out even, go under two bumps on the longer side to compensate. Don't pull the yarn too tightly or you'll end up with a ruffled join. Take the tails to the wrong side, weave them in, and the two pieces will look like one. Magic.

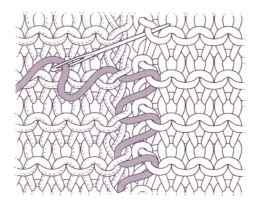

In a side-to-side stitch join, the yarn should weave through the bottom bump on one side, then through the top bump on the matching ridge on the other.

To join two pieces worked in reverse stockinette side to side

This is just like joining two pieces of garter stitch but with twice as many bumps, so it's a bit harder to find the matching rows. Again, with the two pieces placed public side up, catch the bumps at least one half stitch in from the edges so there will be enough yarn in back of the joining yarn to prevent it from showing.

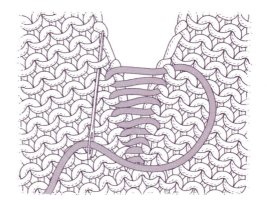

A side-to-side reverse stockinette join is the same as for a garter stitch join, only with twice as many bumps.

The First Stitch of a Seam Is the Most Important One

Why is the first stitch the most important? Because it secures the seam. As with joining, there's more than one way to make that first stitch.

If it's perfection you're after and the first stitch in your seam will be seen by the general public, use the following method to secure it.

If you have a tail hanging from one of the corners, thread it onto a yarn needle. If you don't have a tail to use, cut a piece of yarn at least twice the length of the seam you are planning to sew, plus enough to weave in both ends. If you need more than 18 in., you can pick up another tail from the side seam to continue. Otherwise add in a new piece of yarn.

Place the two pieces next to each other on a flat surface with their public sides facing up and bring the yarn up from the private side in its corner stitch. Take the yarn over to the other piece and bring your needle up from the private side in that corner stitch. Bring your yarn needle up one more time in the corner stitch where you began, creating a figure eight with the yarn, as shown below. Pull the yarn tight to minimize the bulk.

Because this method of joining will never come out after you've hidden the tails, make sure that the edges match each other before you continue. If you've used a new piece of yarn, don't weave the beginning tail in until you're sure that the join is perfect and the garment fits.

If the beginning of a seam is going to be hidden on the inside of a garment or you have a tail with which to start the seam, you can begin a seam by bringing the yarn up in the corner stitch of the other piece.

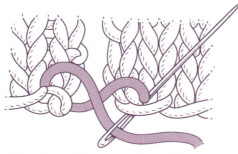

Make a figure 8 for a secure first stitch.

To join two pieces worked in stockinette side to side

The public side of stockinette stitch is made up of rows of Vs. Pull apart the first and second Vs on one edge for a couple of rows. There's a series of horizontal bars in the space you've made. You'll be joining in this space, so you might want to run a lighter thread of a different color under and over these bars so you'll know exactly where to join. Do the same for the other side.

1. With the two pieces placed together, public sides facing out, join the bottom edges, using the method described on p. 86.

2. Now, bring your needle up under the first horizontal bar on the opposite side of where you joined the edge. It should come up between the first and second stitch in the second row.

3. Take your needle to the other side, insert it down into the same space that you first came out of, go under two bars, and bring the needle back up to the public side.

In a side-to-side stockinette join, instead of bumps, you'll be catching bars.

4. Go back to the other edge and insert the needle into the same space that you came up in and bring it up two bars later. Continue in this manner, always going down into the same space that you came up from before. After several rows, pull gently on the yarn until the two sides come together.

If you need to fudge, bring your yarn under one bar only on the shorter side. Of course, you can go under only one bar on each side of the entire length of the join if you want to. When you're finished, take the tails to the wrong side but don't weave them in until you're sure your garment fits.

I'm making a dropped-sleeve sweater. How do I join the top edge of my sleeve to the body?

To do this, you need to use a *side-to-end join*, which is also what you would use to create a fabric from smaller pieces of knitting in which you want to alternate the direction of the knitting, as in patchwork or modular knitting. As with side-to-side joins, the technique you will use depends on the type of stitch you've been knitting.

To join two pieces worked in stockinette side to end

This join won't be quite as invisible as the side-to-side stockinette join, but it will cover up the cast-on or bind-off row. Place the pieces so their public sides are facing up (see p. 86).

1. Bring your yarn or tail up 1 st in from the side of one piece just as if you were going to join two pieces of stockinette side to side.

2. Move across to the piece whose end you are joining, weave the yarn under the two top legs of the first stitch below the cast-on or bound-off edge, and bring the yarn up to the surface. You've scooped the yarn under 1 st.

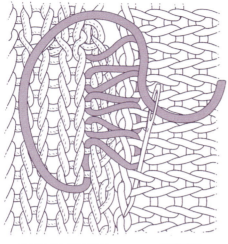

SHOULDER SEAM

BODY OF SWEATER   **SLEEVE**

3. On the piece whose side you're joining, insert your needle down into the space where you started, scoop up the horizontal bar between the 1st and 2nd sts, and come back to the top.

4. Repeat Steps 2 and 3 to continue joining. But, because the stockinette stitch is wider than it is tall, you'll need to go under two horizontal bars every 3 or 4 sts to keep the join even. You can use this to your advantage if you need to fudge.

5. Pull the joining yarn every 4 sts so the pieces come together and the seam disappears.

6. When you come to the end of the join, take the tail to the private side and cut the yarn, leaving a 6-in. tail to weave in.

Tips for Successful Joining

- Make sure you leave long tails when you're knitting, especially at the ends of rows. You can use them for joining the pieces together and you won't have to hide as many tails. If you don't use them, you can hide them in the seams and not worry about them showing.
- Don't join with a length of yarn that is longer than 18 in., as it will wear too much as you weave it back and forth, making it more vulnerable to breaking later on. Fragile yarns or yarns that are loosely twisted need to be even shorter.
- Work the joins in from the edges of your garment because it's almost impossible to fudge at a garment edge if the pieces don't match exactly.
- If the yarn you used to knit the piece is too bulky for joining, use a lighter weight yarn of the same fiber and in the same color. If you can't match the color exactly, a lighter shade is better than a darker one.
- Don't weave the seam ends in until you're sure the garment fits.
- Pin the pieces together first (except when grafting), especially if the seam is a long one. That way, if the pieces are not exactly the same size, you'll be able to compensate as you join.

To join two pieces worked in garter stitch side to end

1. Take the needle (threaded with a tail or piece of yarn) under the bump of the last stitch on the cast-on or bound-off row, as shown in Figure 1.

2. Move to the piece whose end you are joining, weave the yarn under the two top legs of the first V in the row between the cast-on or bound-off edge and the first row of bumps, and pull the yarn through. As you can see in Figure 2, the first leg of this stitch is at the bottom edge.

3. Go back to the piece whose side you are joining and scoop up the next bump (Figure 3).

4. Take the yarn needle to the top piece again and go under the two legs of the next V (Figure 4). Repeat Steps 3 and 4 to continue joining.

5. Pull the joining yarn every 4 sts so the two pieces come together and the seam disappears (Figure 5 on p. 90).

6. When you come to the end of the join, take the tail to the private side and cut the yarn, leaving a 6-in. tail to weave in.

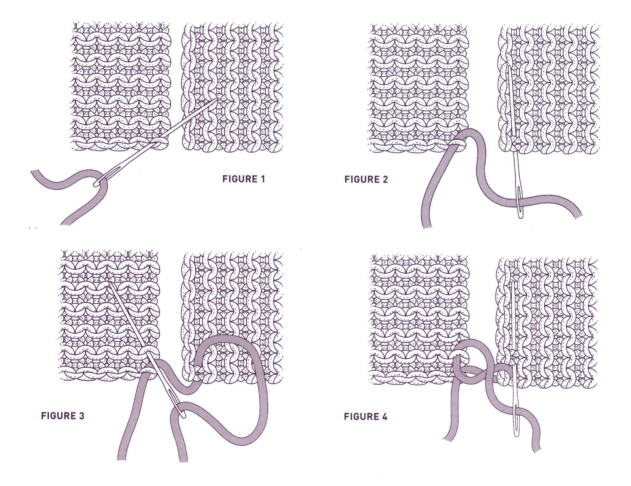

FIGURE 1

FIGURE 2

FIGURE 3

FIGURE 4

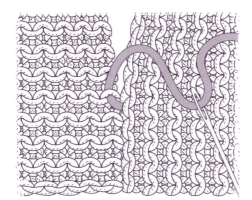

FIGURE 5

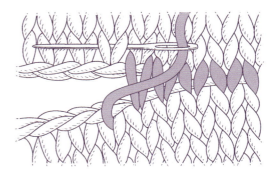

FIGURE 6
Joining two bound-off edges

How do I make all these little squares into strips to make an afghan?

Any time you want all the knitting to go in the same direction, use an *end-to-end join*. This join also works when joining together the shoulders of a sweater.

To join two pieces with bound-off edges end to end

This technique is similar to joining end to side, but, because you're joining pieces end to end, you don't have to compensate for the difference in the height and width of a stockinette stitch. Place the pieces so their public sides are facing up (Figure 6).

1. Bring the yarn up in the middle of the first V above the cast-on or bound-off edge.

2. Insert the needle into the same space on the other piece, under the next two legs of the V and up.

3. Insert the needle on the other side into the same place where you came up, go under the next two legs, and come up. Continue in this manner, always going down into the same stitch that you came up from before so that the joining yarn goes into each stitch twice.

To join two pieces with live stitches end to end

The easiest method for doing this is known as the Three-Needle Bind-Off. In fact, it's so easy that knitters have been known to take out their bind-off rows in order to use it. Because it's very strong, it's good for joining the shoulders of sweaters, as it can support the weight of the yarn below it. Because this seam is decorative on the working side and recessed between the two pieces on the other, you can choose between putting the private or public sides together, depending on the look you want.

Before you begin, make sure you have the same number of stitches on each needle. You also need a third knitting needle of the same size. Figures 7–9 show the join done on the inside of the work with the public sides together.

1. Place one needle slightly higher than the other, with the points of both needles pointing toward your right hand.

2. Take the third needle and insert it into the first loops on each needle as if to knit, as shown in Figure 7. Knit the 2 sts together. Your right needle now has 1 st on it.

3. Knit the next 2 sts together onto the third needle, as shown in Figure 8.

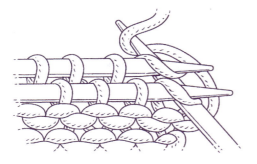

FIGURE 7

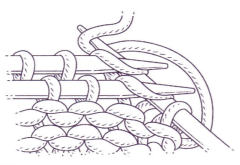

FIGURE 8

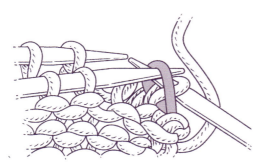

FIGURE 9

4. Insert the point of one of the left needles into the stitch farthest away from the point of the third needle and pull it over the stitch you just finished, as shown in Figure 9. Continue to bind off in this way, knitting 2 sts together from each needle first.

When you finish, the two pieces will be joined with a row of Vs placed end to end on the top.

How do I join two pieces that curve at the edge?

Fold each edge in half and mark the centers with T-pins. Fold each half in half and mark with T-pins. Divide the halves in half as many times as necessary until you have manageable segments. Match up the T-pins and pin the pieces together. Join using the appropriate technique.

How do I "set in" sleeves?

Setting in sleeves involves everything you've learned so far, plus joining two pieces that curve in different ways and are different in length. Before you start, the body pieces should be joined at the shoulders and you need to check that both sleeves match in length and width.

Don't succumb to the temptation of sewing the sides of the sleeve together first because it looks more like a sleeve that way. Doing so makes sewing the sleeve into the armhole infinitely more difficult. Please believe us; we have succumbed and lived to rip. Don't join the side seams first either, as you'll have the same problem.

First, fold the sleeve in half along its length, with the public side facing out, and mark the center at the top of the sleeve with a T-pin. Fold each of these halves together in the same way and mark the centers again with pins. Divide in half as many times as necessary to make it easier to control whatever extra fullness there may be in the sleeve cap. In the same way, divide up the space between the first armhole decreases and the top of the shoulder seam on the front and back and mark with pins. The number of spaces on one half of the sleeve needs to be the same as the number of spaces on the corresponding front or back of the sweater.

With the private sides together, pin the center top of the sleeve to the shoulder seam of the garment, using T-pins. Pin the bound-off stitches of the sleeve to the bound-off stitches of the front and back armholes. Match any

Sleeve and Armhole Ready to Be Pinned Together

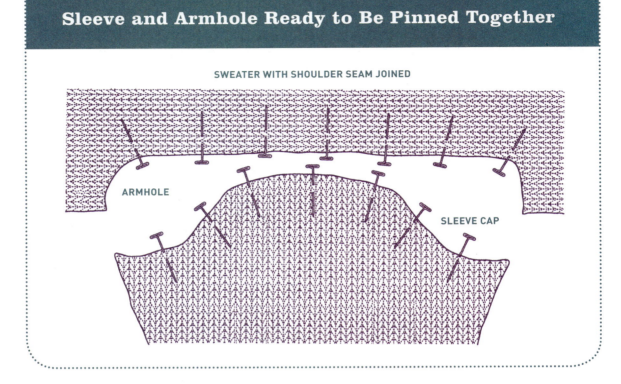

SWEATER WITH SHOULDER SEAM JOINED

ARMHOLE

SLEEVE CAP

increase or decrease rows on the sleeve and body. Then match the remaining pins on the body to the pins on the sleeve and pin them together, easing in any extra fullness.

Follow the directions for joining two pieces with bound-off edges end to end (p. 90) to join each sleeve to the body from the armhole edge to the beginning of the armhole shaping. From that point, use the side-to-side join appropriate to your stitch pattern (pp. 85, 87) until the stitches of each piece are perpendicular to each other. Sew the vertical stitches from one side to the horizontal stitches on the other using the appropriate side-to-end join (p. 90). It is usually a good idea to work from the underarm to the shoulder seam on both sides of the sleeve. This keeps the armholes even and the extra fullness, if any, can be eased along the top of the sleeve.

Once the sleeves are in, you can sew the side seams and the underarm seams. It is a good idea to start from the wrist edge and sew to the underarm, then start again at the bottom of the sweater where the front joins the back and work to the underarm. The edges will match perfectly, and any fudging, if necessary, can be hidden under the arm.

The pattern for my socks says to join the remaining stitches on my toe by grafting them together. How do I do it?
Grafting is yet another way to join live stitches together. When done properly, it is invisible on both sides of the work.

This join takes concentration and some practice, but it's a great status symbol in the knitting world. When you know how to graft, you can boast about it (in an offhand, nonchalant sort of way) and watch nongrafters' eyes widen in admiration.

If that weren't enough reason for you, it's a useful skill to have. Not only does grafting join sock toes, but it is used in lace knitting, for knitting in the round, and for altering a project. Once you learn how to do one type of grafting, the others are a piece of cake.

To graft stockinette

This is also known as the Kitchener stitch, a term that strikes fear and dread into almost every knitter, even those who have never tried it. But the difficulty of its execution has been greatly exaggerated.

Place the two pieces that you're grafting with their private sides together. Arrange the stitches of both pieces on two double-pointed needles. Each needle must have the same number of stitches. Place the back needle slightly above the front one. Grafting goes from right to left, so it's a help if you can arrange the stitches so the tail of your yarn is hanging from the right end of the back needle. (It is possible to start grafting with yarn hanging from any corner, but let's not complicate things.) Thread the tail onto a tapestry needle. If your tail is in the wrong position or not long enough (at least four times the width of the join), thread a new piece of yarn through the second purl bump on the private side under the stitch at the right on the back needle.

The beginning

1. Moving under the two double-pointed needles, bring the tapestry needle in front of both needles and insert it into the first loop on the front needle as if you were going to purl the stitch (Figure 1 on p. 94). Pull the yarn through, leaving the loop on the knitting needle.

2. Take the tapestry needle under the front needle to the back one and insert it into the first loop as if you were going to knit the stitch (Figure 2 on p. 94). Pull the yarn through, leaving the stitch on the needle. It should be snug but not tight.

Kitchener Who?

Lord Horatio Herbert Kitchener was a military hero who served in the British army in the Sudan, the Boer War, and World War I. He worked with the Red Cross to organize British women to knit for the soldiers.

Although no one seems to know whether he was a knitter, he is credited with inventing the grafted toe for closing socks hand-knit from the top down. We speculate that he wanted the socks to have a smooth toe out of necessity; his troops serving in the desert were plagued with blisters caused by the combination of desert sand, heavy boots, and lumpy sock toes. The grafted toe is seamless and far more comfortable.

The Kitchener Stitch

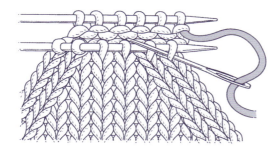

FIGURE 1
Insert as if to purl and leave stitch on front needle.

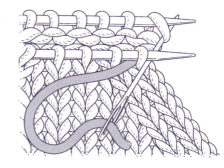

FIGURE 2
Insert as if to knit and leave stitch on back needle.

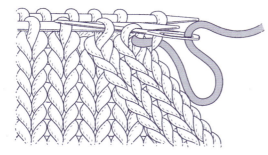

FIGURE 3
Insert as if to knit and remove stitch from front needle. Insert into next stitch as if to purl and leave stitch on needle.

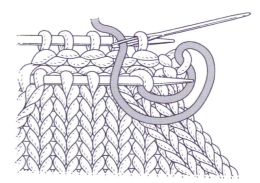

FIGURE 4
Insert as if to purl and remove stitch from back needle. Insert into next stitch as if to knit and leave stitch on needle.

The middle

3. Bring the tapestry needle forward and under the two knitting needles and insert it into the first loop of the front needle as if you were going to knit it and pull the first stitch off the front needle. Continuing on the front needle, insert the tapestry needle in the next loop as if to purl, leaving the loop on the needle (Figure 3).

4. Pass the tapestry needle under the two knitting needles, insert it into the first loop on the back needle as if you were going to purl it, and pull the first stitch off the back needle. Insert the tapestry needle into the next loop on the back needle as if to knit, leaving the loop on the knitting needle (Figure 4).

Notice that there's a pattern in the movements of the tapestry needle as it goes into the stitches: knit, purl on the front needle, then purl, knit on the back. When you've done a few repeats, look back. You've been joining the stitches with a row of Vs that look like knit stitches. That's exactly what they are, knit stitches created with a tapestry needle.

Repeat the middle (Steps 3 and 4) until you have one loop left on each of the knitting needles.

The end

5. Bring the tapestry needle to the front, insert it into the last loop as if to knit, and take the stitch off the needle. Now insert the tapestry needle into the loop that remains on the back needle as if to purl and take off the last stitch. You're finished.

6. Look back at the row of Vs you've made. You may have to tighten or loosen some of the stitches to make this row look just like the rows above and below it. If you haven't grafted the stitches correctly, you'll see it. To make it perfect, you have to pick out the grafting yarn and put the loops back on their respective needles with the correct stitch mount. This is very tedious indeed and if your grafting doesn't look too dreadful, you have our permission to leave it and promise yourself that you'll do better next time.

7. Weave in the tail on the wrong side. Weave in the other tail if you have one.

To graft reverse stockinette

Place the bumpy (public) sides together and use the stockinette graft on the side with the Vs. After you finish, turn your work inside out so that the bumps are on the public side.

To graft garter stitch

Set up your needles with the private sides together and look at the stitches. There should be bumps on the public side right under the front needle. Then look at the private side of the back needle and you should see Vs. If this isn't what you see, you may be able to turn one of the pieces completely around because garter stitch is reversible, switching the private side to the public side or vice versa. But if the pieces can be put together in only one way and the rows under the needles don't come together correctly, you'll need to either pull out or add a row on one of the needles. Or you can put the needles together in the way that makes the most sense to you and live with a join that's not completely invisible but looks quite good anyway.

Once you're ready to begin, start from the right side of the back needle. The process is almost the same as for stockinette.

The beginning

Follow the instructions for grafting stockinette (p. 93), *except* insert your tapestry needle into the first loop of the front needle as if to purl and into the first loop of the back needle, also as if to purl.

The middle

Insert the tapestry needle into the first loop on the front needle as if to knit and take it off. Insert the tapestry needle into the next loop of the front needle as if to purl and leave it on. Repeat this sequence on both needles until you have one loop left on each needle.

The end

Insert the tapestry needle into the last loop on the front needle as if to knit and take off the stitch; repeat with the back needle. Turn the piece over and admire the fact that it looks the same on both sides.

When-It-Doesn't-Fit Emergencies

Okay, you've sewn it up, you've put in the neck, you're ready to try on what you've just put together. Our best thoughts are with you and we fervently hope that it fits you perfectly. If it doesn't, read on.

My sweater is hanging down to my knees. Can it be fixed?
It's easy to take out extra length if the piece has been made in stockinette stitch. You can either totally rip out the extra length and reknit the ribbing, or rip out the extra length and graft the body of the sweater and the intact ribbing together.

Let's start with a total rip out.

1. Measure the length of any special stitches at the bottom (like ribbing) because you'll have to knit this length back onto the sweater.

2. Add this length (if any) to the length you want to remove, measure the sweater, and mark the appropriate row with T-pins.

3. Thread a thinner piece of tightly twisted yarn (mercerized cotton is great) through all the stitches on the row you plan to rip back to or thread a smaller knitting needle through the stitches as you would for ripping (see p. 71).

4. Take out any side joins to about 1 in. above the pins. If you can, leave a long enough piece of yarn to redo the joins.

5. Cut out the cast-on (or unravel the bind-off) row and unravel the yarn until you reach the smaller needle or the piece of yarn marking the row.

6. Put the stitches back on the correct size needle, making sure the stitches are mounted correctly.

7. Turn the piece around so the live stitches are in your left hand. It doesn't matter if the public or private side is facing you as long as you match the stitch pattern of the row below the needle.

8. Reknit the ribbing (if necessary) and bind off.

9. Redo the side joins.

You may have to adjust the number of stitches if your sleeve or body increases started right after the ribbing. Usually you can compensate when you knit the first row of ribbing, but you may have to unravel an additional amount to have enough rows or rounds in which to make the necessary stitch increases or decreases before you begin the ribbing. If you're shortening two identical pieces (sleeves, front/back pieces), make sure that you make the same changes to each.

Don't try the next method until you're familiar with doing alterations and are an experienced grafter.

After you've marked the top row of the alteration with a needle or piece of yarn, choose a row at the bottom of the piece, above the ribbing, without increases or decreases and with the same number of stitches (if possible) as the row you've just marked. Mark this row. If you've used pieces of yarn, replace them with knitting needles. Cut a stitch at the midpoint between the two marked rows and unravel back to both marked rows. You may need to compensate on one piece or the other until you have the same number of stitches on both; graft them together with a piece of the yarn you've unraveled, with the private sides facing each other.

My hand-knit knee socks don't reach my knees (my sweater is too short). What do I do?
Follow one of the methods described in "My sweater is hanging down to my knees," either

ripping back to above the ribbing or ripping out above the ribbing and grafting the ribbing back on when you're done. Once the stitches are secure on the needle, add the necessary rows for the length you want. If you've got enough yarn left over from the same dye lot for the additional length, count yourself lucky. If you don't and you can't locate any more of it, alternate the yarn you've taken out with the yarn from the new dye lot to avoid a slightly off-color stripe.

If you can't locate any of this particular yarn, consider adding a stripe in another color and/or pattern stitch.

Can I shorten or lengthen something not knit in stockinette? What about cables, lace, and color work?

In such cases, it's all about picking the right row. If you're doing cables, pick a row where none of them turn. If you're knitting Fair Isle or an overall pattern in different colors, remove or repeat some of the horizontal bands to shorten it.

We don't suggest shortening or lengthening lace work unless you are a very experienced lace knitter. Even then you can run into trouble.

If you've knit motifs in color work, you may not be able to shorten or lengthen the project without disturbing the overall look. You didn't really want that rabbit's head to come out of his feet, did you?

What can I do if my sweater is too small all over?

Usually the only solution is to reknit, but try being creative first. If you've knit a cardigan, you can add more width to the button side of the band. If it fits on the top but is too tight from the underarm down, you can take out the side seams and knit side panels that taper at the top (so you don't disturb the fit of the sleeves). You might also try taking off the sleeves of the sweater and turning it into a vest.

What happens if I can't get my sweater over my head?

If you think that this is caused by either casting on or binding off too tightly, you need to undo and redo the first or last row.

The most important thing to remember is to start with the last stitch you bound off or the first stitch you cast on. If you can identify the tail, pull it through the last stitch. If it's not possible to do this, cut one of the pieces of yarn in the last stitch. If you can't find the appropriate piece of yarn to tell you what stitch to begin with, cut a stitch in the middle of the row because if you guess and choose the wrong stitch, you won't have an end to sew in without undoing part of the next row. Place the live stitch on a knitting needle. Continue across the row, placing each live stitch on the needle as you free it. If you can't just pull the yarn out (and you can't on most cast-on rows) and you have to cut each stitch, stop when you are 6 sts from the end of the row and unpick the last stitches, because you need enough yarn for a tail to weave in. Check to see that all the stitch mounts are correct. Add another piece of yarn and bind off loosely in pattern, using a larger size needle if necessary. When you weave in the yarn ends, you may have to fiddle a little to make sure the side seams are even.

The top of my ribbing flares and my socks won't stay up. Why?

Your cast-on row and/or ribbing wasn't tight enough. If it's just the cast-on row, follow the instructions for fixing a sweater neck, take it out, and then bind it off tightly on a smaller needle. If it's the ribbing, rip the ribbing back as instructed in "My sweater is hanging down to my knees" and reknit it on smaller needles, taking care to bind off tightly. An easier alternative is to weave a piece of elastic thread through the final row to tighten it up.

Can I fix a hat that is so tight that I can't get it down over my ears?

If the hat is made of a stretchy fiber like wool, we'd try soaking the hat until it's wet and then place it over a bowl that is the same circumference as your head. Otherwise, use the same technique you would use to lengthen or shorten a sweater (see p. 96): Take the work out until you've reached a point at which the hat does fit. Then reknit. Try using a larger needle first and, if that isn't enough, make some increases in inconspicuous places.

There are small holes where I picked up the stitches to knit my neck. Can I hide them?

The easiest way to fix this is to carefully draw the sides of each hole together with a tapestry needle and matching yarn. For next time: When you pick up stitches on a curve, you can avoid holes under your picked-up stitches by not picking up stitches right at the edge. If you pick up a little farther in from the edge, even half a stitch, the top of the edge slides behind the knitting and hides any holes you might make.

My neckline is so big that it's sliding down my shoulder, and I'm not that kind of girl. What can I do?

This is easy to fix if it's a boat neckline. Decide how many inches need to be taken out so it will stay on your shoulders. Divide this number in half and, starting from the place on the neck trim that is over the shoulder join, measure and pin the edges together. Try it on and see if it fits. If it doesn't, move the pins until you're satisfied. Then, with a piece of yarn, carefully sew the excess together from the public side, starting at the shoulder seam so if you decide to change the neck size later you won't have to pull everything out.

If it's a V-neck, the fix is more radical. First, make a guess at how many stitches you will need to take out by pinching the extra fabric together and counting the stitches. Rip back

to the row that you picked up around the neck. If the neck is just a little too big, try reknitting the neck trim with a needle that is at least two sizes smaller than the one you've been using. If you see that this is not going to do the trick or the neck trim has the consistency of cardboard, dump the smaller needle and reduce the number of stitches in the neck edging. How many depends on approximately how many stitches you counted when you pinched the fabric. Because the neckline needs to match on both sides, plan the decreases before you start knitting. Look at the stitches on the needles. Usually you can decrease stitches around the shoulder join in the second row by k2tog at the shoulder joins. Perhaps you can make two decreases on each side of the point of the V. If there are several rows in the edging, you can decrease on every other row or even every row if you're desperate. When you make a decrease on one side, make a matching one on the other so the neck stays even. Keep checking to make sure that the edge doesn't pucker or ruffle. You may have to rip and reknit some to make it look perfect. If you can't make it work any other way, pull out the picked-up stitches and start from scratch. We like to leave the picked-up row in place because ripping out and picking up again can cause holes.

What do I do if the neck of my crew neck looks like a ruffle?

We assume that you've checked the edge and know you can't fix this by tightening up the last row. Before you rip out and reknit, see if weaving some elastic thread through the ribbing will do the trick. If not, follow the instructions for adjusting a V-neck under "My neckline is so big" (at left). If the pattern for the neck trim requires you to pick up a certain multiple of stitches, pick up the number that makes the neck lie flat and either increase or decrease on the next row to get to your multiple as you start the pattern.

Can I fix the bottom ribbing on my sweater if it's hanging, not clinging?

First, try threading a piece of elastic thread through the bottom row or several evenly spaced rows to see if that makes it fit. If that doesn't work, take out the ribbing and reknit the ribbing on smaller needles, making inconspicuous decreases if you need to. If that solution doesn't appeal to you, we have one more suggestion. Take out the side seams, and pull out your sewing machine (or borrow one from a friend or go to a tailor), and sew the side seams back together. If you've used a fine yarn, there might not be too much extra bulk. If it is bulking, use a tight zigzag stitch a little bit outside of where the sweater will be sewn together. That way you can cut off (gulp) the extra bulk without fear.

My sweater is too big all over. Is there a remedy?

You can try controlled shrinking before considering reknitting if:

- The garment is made of a fiber that is at least 50 percent wool.

- You are willing to accept the possibility of it felting and thus becoming permanently too small. (If it does felt, you won't be able to reuse the yarn.)

- You're willing to accept the possibility that, in a multicolored sweater, some of the colors may run.

Since projects made of wool tend to shrink when put in hot water, this is exactly what you're going to do. First, mark the desired measurements on a large piece of paper and put it on top of a couple of towels. Then place the garment in hot water for a minute. Take it out and squeeze out enough water so you can compare it to the measurements on the piece of paper. If it's still too big, repeat the process, never letting the garment rest too long in the water, because you want to avoid felting. As soon as it fits the shape on the paper, pin it out to the correct shape using many pins so the edges will be straight and let it dry.

What is blocking? Is this something I have to do?

Not if you don't want to, but before you decide, let us tell you what blocking does:

- It changes the memory of the yarn from being a ball to being your finished project. This makes stitches more even, helps hide holes and irregularities, straightens edges, and generally improves the project's appearance.

- You can use it to press seams out flat (from the wrong side) if you need to reduce bulk.

- You can use it to change the shape and/or size of what you've made to a certain extent.

The degree of a fiber's flexibility and thus its blockability is determined by what it's made of. Animal fibers are the most flexible; silk fibers less so. Fibers that come from plants, such as cotton, linen, and hemp, are even less flexible.

Contrary to what you might think, synthetics must be blocked with great care. Some melt under the heat of an iron and others become completely limp and stretchy when you pin them out wet. On the positive side, the fact that synthetics resist changing their shape means they often don't need to be blocked.

If your project is knit from a mix of different fibers, read the label of each kind of yarn you used (we *know* you've saved them) for the washing instructions and follow the instructions for the one that requires the most delicate treatment. If you want or need to block and have any reservations about the fiber

Arrange your piece on a blocking board or towel-covered surface according to your desired finished measurements and pin it down in a few places.

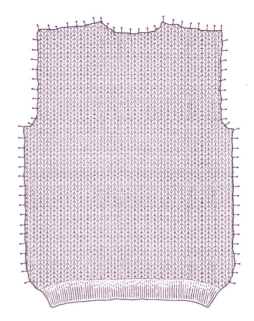

Secure the piece with many pins before proceeding with the blocking.

makeup of your yarn, find the swatch you made and block it first. Of course, if you blocked your gauge swatch before you began to knit, you won't need to do this. Virtue is more than its own reward in this case.

To block, put a towel (or two) on a flat surface a little larger than your project. If you become a blockaholic, you can always buy or make a blocking board, which is marked off in inches and/or centimeters.

Use the finished measurements from the pattern schematic or figure them out from the pattern instructions. If you've changed the measurements, use the new ones. First, pin the corners to the towel or board, then place more pins between the end pins just as you would if you were preparing to join two pieces together (see p. 92).

If you just want to give your piece a new memory or prepare edges for joining, use Blocking Lite. To do this, turn your iron to the

highest steam setting compatible with the yarn content. Place a handkerchief or a dishtowel on top of the knitted piece. Put your iron over the knitting so the steam penetrates both the cloth and the knitting. *Never* rest the iron directly on the knitting! This is especially important when you are blocking ribbing, garter, or any other textured stitch because if the iron rests on the knitting it will flatten the texture, and there is no way to get it back again. Also, if your yarn contains a high percentage of synthetics, you run the risk of melting your knitting, for which there is no known solution. After the steam has penetrated your knitted piece, let it dry completely before you take out the pins.

If, when you take out the pins, the piece snaps back to its original shape, it's time to take sterner measures. Follow the instructions for Blocking Lite but wet the cloth before you place it over the knitted fabric. Hold the iron as close to the fabric as you can without letting its weight rest on the surface, letting the steam from the iron and the moisture from the cloth penetrate the knitting. Never stay in one spot for more than 3 seconds. Let the knitted fabric dry, then unpin it. If this doesn't work, it's time to bring out the big guns.

For Serious Blocking, wet the fabric completely by submerging it in cool water for at least 15 minutes, then take it out, remove as much excess water from it as possible, and spread it out on enough towels to absorb the moisture. Pin it to your desired measurements and let dry completely, replacing wet towels with dry ones. When the knitting is completely dry (don't try to fudge this; you haven't come all this way to take a shortcut that could torpedo the whole undertaking), take out the pins. It's as blocked as it will ever be.

After-the-Knitting's-Done Emergencies

My knitting is dirty; what should I do?
Get out those yarn labels you saved and read them for laundering instructions. Sometimes the label will actually tell you in words how to do this. More often than not, though, it's going to tell you in symbols, so we've given you a laundering decoder ring with "International Laundering Symbols" on p. 102.

If you've used several yarns of different fibers, compare the labels to determine the safest way to handle all of them. If you don't have the yarn labels, dry cleaning is usually your safest bet. It's also the best bet if the fabric you've made is furry or fragile or you're just feeling lazy.

Washing in the machine
Most man-made yarns as well as yarns made of a combination of natural and synthetic fibers can be machine washed. The yarn label should tell you what's safe. For those knitters whose

dogs ate their yarn label, use cool water and wash on the delicate cycle. We always put our knitted items in lingerie bags to protect them from snagging.

It's possible to wash some natural fibers in the machine if you're very careful. If you're not careful, wool can shrink or even felt. Cotton can shrink. Silk tends to become very limp.

Let the machine fill, add whatever you're washing with (we've used baby shampoo, organic shampoo, and products we've gotten from the yarn store, all with success), and lower the item you're washing into the water with both hands. Soak for a few moments if the washing product recommends it. Otherwise, squeeze the knitting gently to release the dirt. Skip the agitation part of the washing cycle. If the yarn is sturdy, you can continue with the draining and the spin. If it's delicate or you're not sure, stop the machine when the tub has drained, take the item out, supporting it with both hands, go past the spin cycle, and let the tub fill up again with the rinse water. Place the garment back in the tub and, depending on the strength of the fiber, leave the item in during the drain and spin or just the drain cycle. If you take the knitting out before the spin cycle, see "Drying" for our way of removing excess water. Frankly, this is almost as much trouble as washing by hand, but we have a feeling (true or not) that things get cleaner if you put them in the washing machine. And washing machines tend to be larger than sinks.

Washing by hand
Fill the basin or tub with cool water and add the washing powder or liquid as directed. Using both hands to support the garment, lower it into the water and allow it to soak for about 5 minutes, unless the washing product tells you otherwise. You can gently squeeze the knitting to release any remaining dirt.

Let the water drain, then pick up the garment with both hands and hold it above the basin to

INTERNATIONAL LAUNDERING SYMBOLS

	Hand wash in lukewarm water only.
	Hand wash in warm water at stated temperature.
	Do not wash by hand or machine.
	Machine wash in warm water at stated temperature, cool rinse, and short spin; delicate handling.
	Machine wash in warm water at stated temperature, short spin.
	Machine wash in warm water at stated temperature.
	Bleaching permitted (with chlorine).
	No bleach.
	Do not dry clean.
	May be dry cleaned with fluorocarbon- or petroleum-based solvents only.
	May be dry cleaned with perchloroethylene or fluorocarbon or petroleum-based solvents.
	May be dry cleaned with all solutions.
	Press with cool iron.
	Press with warm iron.
	Press with hot iron.
	Do not press.
	Do not tumble dry.

allow some of the excess water to run down into the basin. Set it down on a towel while you clean the remaining soap from the basin and refill it with water of the same temperature.

Lower the garment into clean water. Repeat the last two steps until the water is clear.

Drying

We're not fans of machine drying. If you want to try it, make sure you follow the instructions on the yarn label. Watch it like a hawk, checking the dryer every 5 minutes.

To air dry, place the garment on a dry towel after you've rinsed it thoroughly. If it's small enough, you can fold the sides of the towel over it. (Bath sheets are great for this.) Otherwise, put another towel on top. Roll the towels up and press on them to squeeze out moisture. We've been known to put the rolls on the floor and to step on them, pretending we're pressing grapes. Transfer the garment to dry towels and either pat it into shape or pin it out as needed. Let it dry completely (and we mean *completely*). If you don't, the moisture remaining in the garment will distort its shape.

The longer I wear my knitting, the longer it gets. Can I stop this from happening?

Some yarns stretch out as part of their nature. This can also happen if you knit with a heavy yarn. You've got two options:

- You can wash your knitting and put it in the dryer for a few minutes but it may lengthen again when you wear it.

- You can line your garment or have it lined. This works better with a sweater than with a dress.

If you have stretchy yarn in your stash, promise yourself not to use it in a project that's susceptible to stretching.

My garment is pilling, what should I do?

Oddly, synthetic fibers seem to pill the most. There are store-bought solutions, such as sweater stones, sweater combs, and depilling machines, but if you have an electric razor, you can shave the pills off.

Another way to depill is to wind masking or clear tape around your hand, roll your hand over the garment, and lift the pills off. This way you don't have to worry about cutting into the yarn, but it is time and tape consuming.

How do I store my finished handknits?

Always store knitted garments flat, as they tend to grow in length and shrink in width if you hang them up. If you're putting something away for a long time, wash or clean it first. If it's made out of 100 percent man-made yarns, put it in a bag that breathes (plastic or otherwise). But if there is *any* natural fiber in the garment, add cedar balls or your favorite natural moth repellent just in case a moth decides it's found dinner.

I've got a hole in my knitted garment—how do I mend it?

Could the hole be a result of a snag? Go to the wrong side of the garment and see if there is a loop of yarn hanging down. If so, work the extra yarn back into the garment by following the path of the yarn on both sides of the loop and easing it into the surrounding stitches. Be patient. The longer the loop, the more stitches you'll need to ease before it disappears.

If it's not a snag, is the hole in a place where it shows? If not, gather the edges and sew them together with a regular needle, using sewing thread of the same color. Make sure that you catch all the free yarn ends with the sewing thread.

If it's a small hole, but in a prominent location, you may be able to create a duplicate stitch over the hole using the surrounding

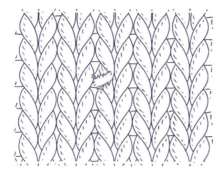

A small hole like this can be repaired using duplicate stitch.

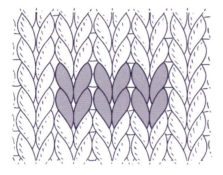

Make a duplicate stitch in the stitch before the hole, one over the hole, and one after the hole. In this example, we did another row of duplicate stitch below it as well.

stitches for stability. With matching yarn and a tapestry needle, start by securing the stitch before the hole by making a duplicate stitch over it (see p. 82); then make a duplicate stitch over the hole, attaching it to the stitch above, and then make another duplicate stitch after the hole. Add more duplicate stitches around the hole as needed to secure the stitch.

If it's a big hole, take it to your yarn store for advice or a referral to someone who specializes in repairing knitted fabric.

The Final Emergency

Now that my project is finished, I don't like it. Is there any hope?
If it's a matter of it not fitting properly, first try the solutions we have offered (see p. 96–99). If it isn't fitting and you can't get it to fit, or you feel it doesn't look good on you, or it's the wrong color, or it just didn't turn out the way you wanted, read on.

Transformation
The first question you need to ask yourself is "Do I like the yarn?" If the answer is yes, think transformation! Free yourself from what the piece was made for. One possibility is to turn a sweater into a pillow by taking out a row under the armholes all the way around (see p. 96), seaming the two edges together using the Three-Needle Bind-Off (see p. 90), stuffing it, and sewing the ribbing together at the bottom. If you want small companion pillows, do the same with the sleeves. If the ribbing pulls together too much, cut it off and do the Three-Needle Bind-Off again at the bottom. Let your imagination run wild!

Recycling
If you're not into transformation, consider recycling the yarn by unraveling it, washing it, and rewinding it. Yarns that can't be recycled are those that break easily and ones that stick to each other (like mohair) as they are worked up. Use your judgment.

If you want to recycle, pick out the joins, if there are any. If you remember in what order you put them together, start with the last join you made and work backward. Starting with the last stitch that you bound off, unravel the yarn and rewind it loosely (because you don't want to stretch it) into balls. Continue until you've unraveled the last stitch.

Borrow a friend's arms or use a chair back to unwind these balls back into skeins. Tie pieces of yarn around the skein in at least four places. The ties should be tight enough to hold the skeins together but should not constrict the yarn. Does your yarn look as if it had a bad permanent? It should.

Wash the skeins following the instructions on the yarn label (see p. 101). Most yarn relaxes during the washing and rinsing process. After the final rinse, press out the extra moisture and put it on a towel or two to dry. If it's still showing a distressing tendency to kink, hang the hank up and attach a small weight to the bottom.

After the yarn is dry, it's ready to be rolled into a ball and knit into something else that will please you more.

I don't like the way the yarn looks; in fact, I never want to see it again. What should I do?
Don't toss it. Just because you don't like what you've made, or it doesn't fit, doesn't mean that all your time and effort is destined for the trash.

- **Give it away to someone who will love and cherish it.**
  What about Uncle Arthur? He likes bright colors and will love the electric blue and acid yellow scarf you thought would look so chic. Plus you won't have to figure out what to get him for his birthday.

- **Give it to someone who needs it.**
  There are many charitable organizations whose sole purpose is to distribute hand-knit items to people who need them. Usually your local yarn shop can help you. If not, at the time of this writing, the Lion Brand® Yarn company has a Charity Connection section on their website.

Having made all these well-meaning suggestions, we empower you to do whatever you want with unwanted projects, even uncompleted ones. But don't feel guilty, whatever you do. You made them and they are yours to dispose of as you see fit.

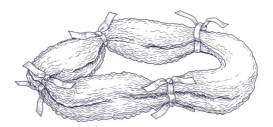
Unraveled yarn looks as if it had a bad perm.

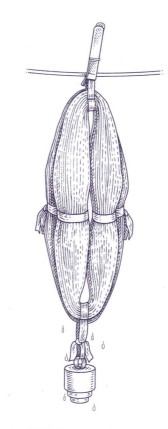
If your yarn is still kinking even after a bath, add a small weight to it as it hangs to dry.

5

Further Adventures in Knitting: Color, Lace & Cables

We've heard from those of you who used the original book (may the Knitting Goddess bless your needles) that you're bored. That's why we wrote this chapter. In it we introduce you to some new techniques, three kinds of color knitting—mosaic, intarsia, and Fair Isle—as well as lace knitting and cables. We'll give you an opportunity to practice your new skills and we advise you on any emergencies that may arise. For those of you who are reading this book for the first time, this chapter is for you, too.

As always, there are many ways to do almost all the new techniques in this chapter, so we're sharing with you the way we do things. Our way is not necessarily the best way or even the "correct" way (according to some knitting purists). So don't feel as if you're doing it "wrong" if you find a better way that works for you. We're not going to rise up from your knitting basket shaking our fingers at you.

Color Knitting

Color knitting is not difficult to learn. If you can knit and purl, you'll be able to knit as though in Technicolor if you choose (especially if you use variegated yarn). You do have to concentrate a little more, especially at first.

MOSAIC KNITTING

We begin with what we think is a really easy type of color work, mosaic knitting. We love mosaic knitting because:

- You only work with one color in each row.

- It's fast. You only have to look at the chart every other row.

- Changing or altering a mosaic pattern is fun and easy.

- It gives you a lot of bang for your buck. The finished objects look impressive and make good last-minute gifts. We like to make home goods like coasters and potholders and pillow covers, as well as fashionable items such as the Mosaic Mitts on p. 133.

- You can insert a mosaic pattern into plain knitting to make your project look more complicated.

Okay, now that you are sold on this technique, let's get started. To practice, we'll use the Mosaic Mitts Chart (see the full pattern on p. 134). It's different from most charts that you come across in color knitting. In mosaic knitting, every charted row is worked twice, once from right to left, and then back from left to right—even though there is only one row on the chart. To remind you of this, there is a number 1 on the right side of the first charted row and a number 2 on the left side of that same row. You'll knit all the stitches of one color as you go, and slip all the stitches of the other color. After you turn back, you work the same row on the chart again but from left to right. On the private side, knit the knit stitches and slip the slipped ones. *Always slip stitches purlwise.*

Mosaic Mitts Chart

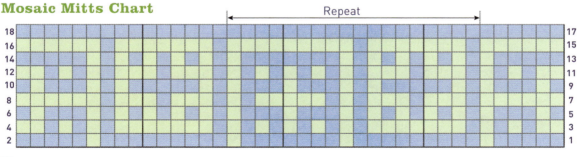

Key

Darker color, Cruise ("D")

Lighter color, Spruce ("L")

Let's practice. De-stash two contrasting colors (L and D) of the same yarn and determine the appropriate sized needles, or use the suggested yarn and needles from the pattern on p. 133.

Using the long-tail method, cast on 39 sts using the lighter color (L) and knit 3 rows.

You'll begin mosaic knitting on Row 1 of the chart (see p. 107).

Mosaic Chart Row 1, worked right to left (number 1, p. 107)

Using yarn D, k5, sl1p, k9, sl1p, k7, sl1p, k9, sl1p, k5. Turn.

In other words: Using yarn D (see the dark square?), look at the chart and knit all the dark stitches and slip all the light stitches as if to purl. After knitting the last stitch, turn. Remember: *Always slip stitches so that the working yarn remains on the private side.*

Mosaic Chart Row 2, worked from left to right (number 2, p. 107)

There is no need to drive yourself crazy by trying to read the second half of the row backward. Look at your knitting instead.

Knit the D stitches and slip the L stitches as if to purl. Because we're using garter stitch, bring the D yarn to the private side before each slipped stitch and back to the public side after the slipped stitches. This keeps the yarn on the private side where it belongs. Mosaic knitting is meant to be seen from the public side only. The private side is really ugly because you always slip the stitches on the private side.

The next row of the chart (numbers 3 and 4)

Start with yarn L this time, knitting the L stitches and slipping the D stitches. Turn your work and follow your knitting as indicated.

Work your way up the chart to the top of Row 17/18, which is all knitted in yarn D.

If you're going to finish the Mosaic Mitts, follow the instructions as written on p. 134. If you don't want to make the mitts, you can just practice mosaic knitting with the chart. We marked the repeat for you so you can make your sample as long as you like. A belt, anyone? Or, perhaps a bell cord to ring when summoning your loved one? To finish your practice piece, knit 3 more rows in L and bind off.

How can I easily make variations to mosaic patterns?

The Mosaic Mitts chart pattern—and other mosaic patterns—can be easily changed to create different looks. Here are a few of our favorite methods:

- Switch the colors.

- Work purl stitches on the return half of each row.

- Work garter stitches, but always leave the yarn in the front of the slipped stitches—or use purl stitches and do the same. This design element came from one of our best mistakes.

- Turn any chart upside down and work it from "top" to "bottom."

Now that we've gotten your creative juices going, we're sure you can think of more variations. For more patterns, refer to Barbara Walker's *Mosaic Knitting* (see p. 154) or make them up yourself.

NEW TECHNIQUES FOR COLOR KNITTING

Now we'd like to introduce you to two techniques that will make intarsia and Fair Isle

Design Secrets

When you are ready to design your own mosaic chart, use the following conventions:

- You can never slip a stitch upward for more than two rows.
- Begin and end each row with the color with which you're knitting the row. This way there won't be any slipped stitches at either end of the row and you'll know what color to begin knitting with.

Some designers don't follow these design conventions, but we stick with our idol, Barbara Walker. We think the finished piece looks better and, most of the time, we hide the extra stitches on each side into the seam. We consider ourselves Mosaic Knitting Purists.

much easier for you to knit. You'll find many other uses for these techniques as well. If you'd like to skip learning them, be our guests, but we bet you'll come back to them later on.

Ambidextrous knitting, or learning how to knit with your other hand

If you choose to learn only one new knitting technique from this chapter, this is the one.

As knitting horizons have broadened, knitters have come to realize that there are many ways to knit. If you've learned to knit from an American or a Brit, you'll throw the yarn over the needle with the right hand. If you've learned from a European, you'll hold the yarn with the left hand, usually called Continental knitting. When we teach people how to knit, we wait and see which hand is easier for the knitter to use. This makes us feel very liberal and up-to-date.

There is great controversy over which is the *best* way to knit. We don't have to choose sides (luckily) because we knit with both hands, separately and together.

Why would I want to learn to knit with my other hand? It was hard enough to learn with one hand.

- It forces you to go back to that beginner's mind-set, which is very good for humbling one's Inner Knitting Snob.

- It makes it much easier to knit with two or more colors.

- When you learn a new technique such as knitting backward (see p. 111), you can try using either hand to discover which way is easier for you.

- It gives you the ability to knit with the yarn in *either* hand, which you will find very useful.

- Most important, if the hand that usually holds the yarn is out of commission for any reason, you don't have to stop knitting! Just switch hands.

Your last point convinced me. I never want to stop knitting.
Now that you're convinced that it's worth a try, begin a practice swatch by casting on 20 sts and knitting 3 rows in your usual fashion. If you cast on 30 sts, you'll eventually have a very strange-looking scarf, and you can give it to that person who is always nagging you for a handmade scarf that you have no intention of knitting. The person will never ask again.

We've included instructions for righties who want to knit left-handed and lefties who want to knit right-handed. Choose the way that applies to you.

Left-handed knitting for the right-handed

At the end of the 3rd row of your practice swatch, turn and pick up the working yarn with your left hand. You may find that copying the way you hold the yarn in your right hand translates easily to holding it in the left. If not, try this: Wrap the working yarn around your little finger, bring it toward you, up and in front of the ring and middle fingers and then over your index finger.

Not only does this feel awful, but my working yarn is flopping all over the place.
Relax; many things that are new feel awful at first. Pull back on the yarn that comes from the ball until you have tension. If you're able to keep the yarn between the tip of the first finger and the first joint (and you will with practice), you'll have more control over it.

The knit stitch
Now that you are in position with tension on the working yarn, take a few deep breaths.

Put your right needle through the stitch as usual. With your left hand bring the working yarn over the right needle from left to right. (This is exactly the same motion that you are accustomed to making with your right hand.)

Pull the working yarn through the stitch with the right needle. You now have a new stitch on the right needle so release the old stitch from the left needle in your accustomed manner.

Keep knitting with the yarn in your left hand until you've reached the end of the row, then turn and continue to use your left hand until you're fairly comfortable. After a while you can try "scooping" the working yarn with your right needle while keeping it under tension as described above. This method will increase your knitting speed.

I'll never get used to this. Keep practicing. Rome wasn't knit in a day.

The purl stitch
After you've got "left-handed knitting" under your belt, you're ready to learn how to purl.

The next time you turn your work, purl back about 5 sts as you normally would. The yarn is in front of your work. Holding the yarn in your left hand (you should be an old pro by now), put your right needle into the stitch as if to purl. Take the working yarn with the left hand and wrap it counterclockwise over the right needle. Push the loop that has appeared on the top of the right needle through the center of the stitch you're purling. The new stitch appears as if by magic on your right needle, so push the old stitch off the left needle.

Again, repeat until you've reached the end of the row, turn, and continue to purl with your left hand. Practice. You can even knit one row and purl one row for a while and then knit one stitch, purl one stitch.

Right-handed knitting for the left-handed

Follow the "Left-Handed Knitting" instructions for beginning your swatch. At the end of the 3rd row, turn, knit 5 sts with your left hand, and pick up the working yarn with your right hand.

If copying the way you hold the yarn in your left hand translates easily to holding it in the right, you are ready to knit. If not, try wrapping the working yarn around your little finger, bring it toward you, up and in front of the ring and middle fingers, and then over your index finger.

The knit stitch

Take a few deep breaths before you begin, and then just put your right needle through the stitch as usual. With the right index finger, swing the working yarn counterclockwise over the right needle. Pull the right needle (with the working yarn on top of it) through the stitch. You now have a new stitch on the right needle, so release the old stitch from the left needle as you usually do.

Keep knitting with the yarn in your right hand until you've reached the end of the row, turn, and continue to knit with your right hand until you're fairly comfortable with it.

You're kidding. I'll never get used to this.

Practice, practice, practice. You do want to knit on the stage of Carnegie Hall, don't you?

The purl stitch

With "right-handed knitting" checked off your to-learn list, you're ready to learn how to purl with your right hand.

The next time you turn your work, purl back about 5 sts using your left hand. The yarn is hanging in front of your work.

Holding the yarn in your right hand, put your right needle into the stitch as if to purl. Use your right index finger to guide the working yarn and wrap it counterclockwise over the right needle. Push the loop that has appeared on the top of the right needle through the center of the stitch you're purling. It now appears on your right needle, so pull the old stitch off the left needle.

My tension is really, really off.

Of course it is. Your tension will get better with practice. If you practice knitting and purling with the opposite hand for only five minutes a

day, *every* day, your hands will soon become familiar with the motions and, gradually, your tension will settle down—just as when learning to knit the first time around. This learning process will make you forever patient with those who are learning to knit for the first time.

Once you're comfortable knitting with the other hand, you may want to switch to using it all the time. Some of us do, some of us don't.

Shift into reverse, or working backward

Working backward is the second technique we want to show you to make your color knitting easier. If you just can't wait any longer to knit in color, you can skip over to the intarsia section on p. 113 for now, but we'll bet you'll be back. The rest of you, read on.

Why in the world would I want to knit or purl backward?

- You can see exactly what you are doing when knitting complicated color charts because this technique enables you to always face the public side of your work.

- You don't have to keep turning your piece around when working a few stitches in one direction and then a few in the other, as when making sock heels or narrow strips of knitting.

Knitting backward for garter stitch

If you knit forward and then knit backward, you'll have two rows of garter stitch.

Cast on to begin a practice swatch and knit a few rows as usual. When you are ready, finish a row but don't turn your work. Bring the yarn to the front as if to purl.

Poke the left needle, back to front, through the center of the first stitch on the right needle. The left needle should be under the right one, pointing toward you through the legs of this stitch. Wrap the working yarn counterclockwise around the front needle and push back the

Knitting Backward and the Streamer Scarf

Marion realized the benefits of knitting and purling backward when she made her first Streamer Scarf, which she envisaged as a scarf made up almost entirely of long pieces of knitted fabric to be wrapped and arranged any which way (and no doubt do some "streaming" in the wind). She cast on all six streamers in different colors on her needle and tried to work across, but untangling the different balls of yarn made her crazy. Then she had a Knitting Flash. Why not knit each streamer separately? This adjustment made the work better, but she quickly tired of turning her work. She had another Knitting Flash: *Why not knit backward every other row?*

Flush with genius, Marion taught herself how to do it through trial and error. Of course, she didn't know then that this technique has been around for a long time. If you'd like to make the latest version of the Streamer Scarf and practice knitting and purling backward, the pattern is on p. 138.

strand that is now between the needles. That strand will go through the old stitch and end up on your left needle. Repeat across the row, and repeat some more.

The bumps face you as you knit backward from left to right.

Purling backward for stockinette stitch

If you knit forward and purl backward, the result will be stockinette stitch.

Finish a row on your practice swatch but don't turn your work. Make sure that the yarn is in back of the needle.

Poke the left needle from front to back between the two legs of the next stitch on the right needle. Bring the working yarn in a counterclockwise direction over the left needle, all the way to the back. With the left needle, bring the new stitch through the loop and onto

the left needle and release the old stitch from the right needle.

The purl bumps will be on the back of the work as you purl backward from left to right.

I can't understand your instructions.

There is another way to learn to knit backward without instructions. You may find it easier and it works with both knit and purl stitches. It's especially useful if you suddenly need to work backward and can't remember how you did it the last time. We find it ironic that this method forces you to turn your work in order to learn how *not* to turn it.

This method reminds us of The Byrds hit "Turn! Turn! Turn! (To Everything There Is a Season)." It's an oldie but goody.

1. Turn the work and start knitting or purling back on the private side in the usual way.

2. After about 5 sts, put the right needle through the stitch as usual.

3. Turn the work around to the public side and notice where the needle is placed.

4. Turn the work back to the private side and wrap the yarn.

5. Turn the work to the public side and see how you've wrapped the yarn over the needle.

6. Turn the work to the private side and pull the loop of the new stitch partly through the old stitch.

7. Turn the work to the public side, note where the yarn is, and pull the new stitch through the old.

Now take it from the top (if you remember all the steps). If you forget, turn the work around, start the next step and turn back again.

Hopefully all this discomfort will help you remember all the steps and you can work from the front. The turning and turning is negative reinforcement for a positive result.

INTARSIA, AKA COLOR BLOCK KNITTING

Some people call this technique Color Block Knitting, which we must admit is very descriptive; however, we prefer to use the word *intarsia* because it sounds fancier.

Intarsia is traditionally defined as working with several colors in a single row, each color kept in its own area. Every time there is a color change, you start a new piece of yarn. Think of a row of bunnies knit along the bottom of a child's cardigan, or a portrait of your cat knit into the front of your sweater. Intarsia is usually knit in rows so the yarn will be in the correct place the next time you come to it. It's not impossible to knit intarsia in the round, but it's

complicated and beyond the scope of this book.

Most patterns use charts to show you which colors to use (see "A Sample Color Chart" on p. 44). The areas knit in different colors may range from a single stitch to a shape many stitches wide and many rows high. Generally, the more colors used, the more difficult the intarsia pattern is to knit. The pattern for the Pillow of Many Colors on p. 140, minus the Fair Isle section in the middle, is a sample of very easy intarsia because you change colors only once a row.

How can I change colors along the row when I only have one ball of yarn of each color?
You can cut lengths of yarn from each ball and use them as you come to each differently colored square on the chart. There's a very complicated way of figuring out how long each length should be, but we don't use it. However, if you want to try it, wind the yarn around the needle for each stitch you will make (after you count them, of course) and then add 12 in. for the tails (6 in. each), a little more for good luck, and then cut. We don't feel that this way is worth the time. We think that the length of yarn should be determined by how you manage all the strands, whether by bobbin or by strands of free-floating yarn. We call these methods the Ahza Way and the Marion Way.

To follow the Ahza Way, wind a bobbin for each instance of a color in a row. (You can wind quite a lot of yarn on each.) Then, as you work across each row, simply select the correct bobbin, unraveling more yarn as you need it. Every row or rows, hold your knitting upside down and shake out the tangles in the bobbins. They will always hang on the purl side.

For the Marion Way, cut long strands of each yarn (about a yard or so for each color) and let them hang free on the private side of the work. After every row, run your fingers through the strands, so they hang down straight. If you run out of yarn, just attach another length. Of course, this means you may have more ends to weave in, but at least the clacking of bobbins will never drive you nuts.

Changing colors in a row

Traditionally, changing from one yarn to another is done on the private side of the work, and the color changes often happen on every row. If you've learned to knit backward, discussed on p. 111), use the technique here. You'll find that it's easier to keep track of which color to use next because you are always looking at the work from the public side, just the way the color chart is written. If, however, you are turning your work and are on the private side, it's more challenging to see what the row is supposed to look like. When you change from one color to another in a single row, the strands need to be wound around each other at each color change (Figures 1 and 2).

Working from right to left on the public side, knit your last stitch in the first color and make sure that both the first and next color are hanging down behind your knitting. Place the yarn you were using over the new color. Then bring the strand of the new color around and over the strand that you were knitting with. Drop that old strand and knit on using the new color as the working yarn. Do this at every color change across the row. At the end of the row, either knit backward or turn the work. If you've turned the work and are now on the private side, do exactly the same thing when changing colors, but make sure that both colors are hanging on the private side.

Keep placing old over new, new over old.

I'm knitting with multiple colors and I have slits showing where the colors change. What do I do now?

These slits appear when the new working yarn has not been wrapped around and over the previous color at the change. We've discovered only two solutions to this problem. The easiest one is to frog to the first slit, wrap the yarns as instructed in "Changing Colors in a Row" and reknit. The second solution is to use a sewing needle and thread or thin piece of yarn to sew the slits together. As a warning, it's difficult to make the public side look good when sewing together the slits, and you end up with even more ends to weave in. If you *really* don't want to reknit, you could always try to make those slits into a design element!

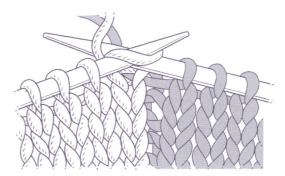

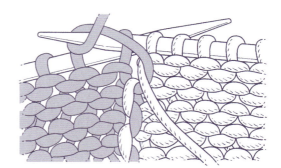

FIGURES 1 & 2
Here is the transition from one color block to the other (top). You can clearly see on the purl side (bottom) how the working yarn wraps around and over the dropped yarn.

FAIR ISLE KNITTING

Believe Marion when we tell you that Fair Isle is easier to knit than intarsia. Or, believe Ahza, who thinks it isn't.

Fair Isle consists of horizontal bands of color, sometimes separated by plain rows or small horizontal patterns. The patterns in the bands

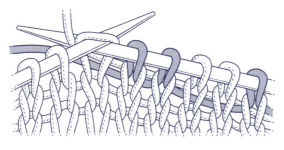

FIGURE 3
Carrying two colors on a knit row.

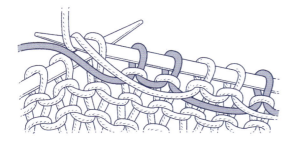

FIGURE 4
Carrying two colors on a purl row.

are geometric and fairly abstract. No little bunnies here. There are some all over patterns in Fair Isle, but they are few and far between.

The rows that have more than one color (two colors, traditionally) are worked by carrying the two colors all along the row. This process is a type of stranded knitting. Carrying the yarn that you are not knitting with across the row is not confined to Fair Isle; that is why we call it a type of stranded knitting.

Tension is king (or queen) in Fair Isle. If tension isn't consistent, some of your stitches will bunch up and some will be very, very loose. Unless your pattern absolutely tells you otherwise, do your swatch in a Fair Isle pattern. The gauge is strikingly different from plain vanilla stockinette.

Fair Isle is worth learning because it looks quite complicated but is easy to do.

- Each row of the pattern is worked in two colors only, and they are both carried along behind the row (stranded knitting). However, you don't need to use the *same* two colors in every row. In Pillow of Many Colors on p. 140, there are five colors in the Fair Isle Section.

- The pattern often changes from row to row, even though these rows may be repeated. Of course, this is another reason why knowing how to knit backward (p. 111) will make your knitting life better. It's good to be able to see the public side all the time when rows feature complex patterning.

- Traditional Fair Isle patterns are designed so that you don't have to carry the unused color more than 5 sts, so loops of yarn on the private side are not a problem and, if you do it right, you won't be able see the yarn that is not in use from the public side.

At the risk of boring you, this is one reason why you learned how to knit with the opposite hand. This enables you to work with each hand carrying a strand of yarn (see p. 109). If you haven't learned this technique by now, go back and learn it. The alternatives are very slow going and involve a lot of yarn shuffling.

Learn Fair Isle by knitting the Fair Isle section from the Pillow of Many Colors Chart on p. 143. Cast on 44 sts and knit several plain rows. When you are ready, begin the chart, stranding the yarn colors as you go.

We hold the background color in our right hand and the pattern color in our left hand. We do this on every row, and we mean *every*. That way you'll always know which yarn is supposed to go in which hand. And the finished piece will look better; you can take our word for it. If you don't want to take our word for it, here's the explanation. Bands with the same pattern in the same two colors look different depending

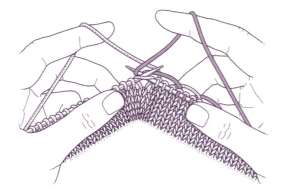

FIGURES 5
Knitting with right-hand yarn.

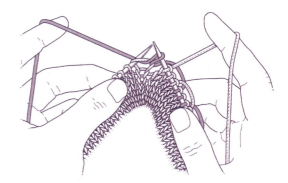

FIGURES 6
Knitting with left-hand yarn..

on which yarn you hold in which hand. Try it and you'll see the difference.

When the background color is stranded over the pattern color (the background color is held in the right hand), the pattern stitches show up more. When the background yarn is stranded underneath (held in your left hand), the pattern stitches will be less noticeable.

It's not a good idea to switch the position of the two yarns from row to row. The resulting pattern will look confusing to the eye. Even worse would be to switch yarn positions in the same row. (Perhaps you left your knitting before you finished the row?)

Some knitters, and you may be among them, prefer to hold the background color in the left hand, and that's okay. Just be consistent so that your pattern looks consistent, too.

I used the wrong color about 10 rows back. Can I fix this terrible mistake?
Don't worry about it. We have three solutions.

1. Live with it, or repeat the "mistake," making it a design element.

2. Work along your row until you are above the stitch that precedes the mistake. Unravel the stitches all the way down the column of stitches until you reach that mistake, and then reknit the stitches using the correct yarn until you're back at the top. Of course you need to look at the chart on the way up. The correct yarn is stranded behind the offending one; you can knit in the correct color and let the wrong one lie in back.

3. Take a piece of yarn in the correct color and make a duplicate stitch (see p. 82) over the mistake.

Knitting Fair Isle in the round
The sample Fair Isle swatch that you practiced on from Pillow of Many Colors on p. 143 is knit back and forth. Fair Isle can also be knit in the round on circular or double-pointed needles. Knitting in the round allows you to read the pattern chart from right to left on every row (round) because you are always knitting on the public side. Fair Isle in the round is great for knitting hats, socks, and pretty much anything that is shaped like a tube. Perhaps you'd like to make a warmer for your favorite wastebasket.

What kind of yarn should I use?
When choosing yarn for that wastebasket warmer or holiday sweater, look for 100 per-cent wool. Its elasticity makes it easy to use, especially when you're learning, and the

stitches will even out considerably when the piece is blocked. Traditionally, Shetland yarn is the yarn of choice because it offers good stitch definition. A Fair Isle pattern in mohair would look like a big hairy mess.

Remember that stranding essentially creates an extra layer of yarn on the private side of a garment. This attribute is great for winter warmth, but Fair Isle does not make it a good choice for a summer sweater.

Even though we've presented the types of color knitting separately, sometimes these techniques are used together. Intarsia often uses stranded knitting, a technique used by Fair Isle.

Let's take as an example that child's sweater we conjured at the beginning of this section—the one with all those bunny rabbits across the bottom. Say you have six bunnies with two blue eyes each, and each bunny's eyes are 2 sts apart. If you cut a new piece of blue yarn for each eye, you'd have 24 ends to weave in. Ridiculous. What if you decided to carry the yarn for the blue eyes across the row from the first eye to the last one? Wouldn't that be easier?

My color is not where it's supposed to be. What do I do?

When knitting with multiple yarns, it's a good idea to pay attention to where you're going to need each yarn strand next. You could start a new yarn every time you needed a particular color, but then you'd have even more ends to weave in.

Instead, move the color to where it will be needed next by catching it every 3 to 5 sts. That's stranded knitting, carrying two or more yarns across the row. (For more on stranded knitting, see "Fair Isle Knitting" on p. 114.)

There are two ways to carry yarn: the easy way or the hard way. The easy way assumes that you have learned to carry the yarn with both hands (see p. 109). And the hard way—well, we really, really want you to learn to carry the yarn in both hands.

If you're knitting

Make sure that the background yarn is in your right hand and the contrasting yarn that you want to catch (we call it the *floating yarn*) is in your left. Secure the floating yarn by bringing it above the background yarn and knitting 2 sts. Bring the floating yarn back down over the background yarn and keep knitting. The floating yarn is caught by the next stitch.

If you're purling

Again, with the background yarn in your right hand and the floating yarn in your left, bring the floating yarn up and to the right-hand side of the right needle, purl over it for 2 sts using the background yarn, and then move the floating yarn back down.

That's all there is to it. Catch the yarn every 3 to 5 sts with the background color as you go along. The number of stitches that you can skip without creating loops along the private side of the fabric varies with the thickness of the yarn you're using (and your personal compulsivity). That's why 3 sts is the low end of our stitch-catching spectrum. As for the high end, if you skip more than an inch of stitches—whatever the thickness of yarn or your gauge—you'll be sorry.

There are more complicated ways to secure the floating yarn and, if you are curious or a strict traditionalist, you can learn about them in the general books we've listed in "Further Reading" on p. 154.

How do I change colors when knitting stripes?

If you've never used the new color before, start a new piece of yarn. If you're changing colors at the edges every 3 or 4 rows, hold the yarn(s) you're not using in front of the new working yarn, then bring the new yarn under the yarn(s)

you're carrying and start to knit. Knit across the row in your pattern. As you work, you'll move the yarn strands along the edges to the next place they are used in the pattern. To move 4 or fewer rows, just loosely pick up the appropriate strand as instructed.

If a yarn doesn't come back into use after 4 rows, wrap it together with the working yarn to prevent loops or puckers from forming, and carry the yarns as you go (Figure 7). Make sure that the yarn is being carried up the edges loose enough so the sides don't pull up, but not so loose that you end up with loops.

You can carry more than one color at a time, but if it looks like you've added a rope to the side of your knitting or you've worked more than 5 rows, you should drop the extra strand or strands and resign yourself to cutting the yarns and weaving in more ends.

There are those who swear by their most intricately knitted socks that all the wraps mentioned above *must* be done in the opposite direction from what we've already described, bringing the next strand over, not under, the strands not in use. So be it. We're not looking to start a fight. If you are consistent, wrapping in the same way throughout the project will work fine.

Knit in peace.

Why do I have to catch all these floats?

Keeping an even tension is probably the most important thing when knitting with multiple yarns. If you pull the floats too tight, whatever you're knitting will have puckers in it. If the floats are two loose, well, just wait until you wear your new sweater, a masterpiece of color knitting, for the first *and last* time because one of those loops catches on an earring and stretches the stitches out of shape.

Can't I catch the yarn that I'm carrying behind the stitches for one stitch?

Only if you want to risk this yarn showing

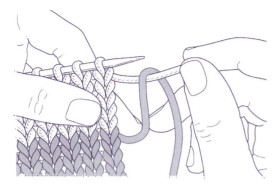

FIGURE 7
Wrapping yarn vertically

through to the public side. We're not quite sure why you'd want to do this, but you're welcome to try any way you wish.

What do I do with all these yarn strands that dangle from my knitting?

The best way to get rid of ends is to weave them in as you go. To do this, weave the new yarn in back of the working yarn for about 2 in. before your color change, leaving a 6-in. tail. When weaving, use the technique for catching floats, wrapping the yarn every other stitch.

It's essential that you leave a 6-in. tail because when you are working the next row, you'll weave that tail in the opposite direction—and you don't want to run out of yarn. By the time you've woven that yarn tail 2 in. along one direction and 2 in. along the opposite direction, there's no way it will come out, and you can trim the remaining end.

This technique works very well with finer yarns, but if you begin to notice ridges on the public side, stop. You'll have to sew in the ends in this case.

Help! I have snagged one of the floating strands on my finished sweater. What do I do?

Carefully unwind the yarn from the earring (or whatever has snagged it). Turn the sweater public side up and assess the damage.

If just one stitch has disappeared, you can gently pull on it with a tapestry needle and it will come back into view. If surrounding stitches are also pulled out of shape, even them out by pulling the side of the stitches with a tapestry needle. You'll learn a lot about stitch construction as you figure out where to pull the yarn.

But I broke the yarn when the sweater snagged, and the ends are too short to weave in. Is there no hope?

Cut a 12-in. piece of the yarn you knit your sweater with (or as close to the same yarn as you can get) and thread your tapestry needle with it. Leaving a 4-in. tail, use the repair yarn to make a duplicate stitch (see p. 82) over the broken stitch or stitches. If the repair doesn't show too much, leave the old yarn in to bond with the new yarn the first time you wash it. Otherwise, you'll need to duplicate stitch over enough of the original color yarn to be able to weave in the loose, broken ends. In any case, you'll have to weave in the ends of the new yarn.

Lace Knitting

Lace is knit across the world, and regions have developed their own particular styles. Even Alaska has its own style of lace knitting. In our opinions, as soon as you have learned to knit, purl, increase, and decrease, you are ready to knit lace. For the beginning lace knitter, we feel it's easier (and much faster) to alternate plain rows with lace pattern rows, which makes our Lace Sampler Wrap pattern in Chapter 6 the perfect first project.

As simple as lace knitting can be, there are some special qualities that you may want to cultivate as a lace knitter. We call them the "Three Ps":

- **Pickiness**

  Knitting lace is exacting. There is no room for error. The smallest mistake can ruin the whole look, and you can't "design" your way out of it. In the beginning you'll have to pay attention closely. As you become more expert, you'll be able to memorize the pattern and relax a little.

- **Patience**

  You'll need patience to frog (rip out) your work back to a mistake and then reknit, and it is not that easy to pick up the stitches again. (Never fear, we have a tip for that!)

- **Possession**

  (as in lots of stitch markers and blocking pins): Owning lots of different stitch markers in lots of different colors allows you to separate groups of stitches, so you don't have to count the whole row or round all at once. Also, unwaxed dental floss should be added to your Tool Kit, as should more T-pins for blocking.

Lace has holes in it. And yarn overs make holes. Therefore, it is the yarn overs that make knitted lace. If you need a refresher yarn overs (YO), you can review them on p. 49.

The openness of a knitted lace fabric depends on the thickness of the yarn, the number of yarn overs in a row, and the relationship between the size of the yarn and the needle diameter.

Imagine knitting lace with a sport weight yarn and size 15 needles (U.S.). Your piece will have very large holes. If you knit the same pattern using the same yarn but use size 1 needles (U.S.) instead, the result will be a very dense piece of knitting with very tiny holes.

Another characteristic of yarn overs is that they increase the total number of stitches in the row. When you knit into the yarn over on the next row, you've made a hole below and increased a stitch above. This is great when you want to work a triangle shawl that has more and more stitches in each row and widens and widens until you just can't stand it anymore and bind off.

Lace Knitting vs. Knitted Lace

The "lace knitting" versus "knitted lace" debate has been long standing among knitters. Are these two different kinds of lace? Or just one with two names? It all boils down to how often you knit a pattern row. Many people say that lace knitting refers to knitting a pattern row on *every row*, and knitted lace alternates pattern rows with plain rows of knit or purl.

There seems to be no historical basis for this distinction, although many knitters have decided opinions. Certainly neither is "purer" than the other, and we use the terms interchangeably.

But if you want to make something that is square or rectangular (such as our Lace Sampler Wrap on p. 144), you must balance each increase by making a decrease in the same row. This decrease ensures that your overall stitch count will stay the same. The decreases can be right next to the increases or far away.

There are exceptions to the rule that every increase is balanced with a decrease, but if the stitch count varies intentionally from row to row it should be clearly marked in the pattern.

We strongly suggest that you count your stitches early and often to make sure the pattern is correct. An error that doesn't look too visible immediately will look increasingly bad as you continue knitting. The mistake follows you in every succeeding row and laughs at your feeble attempts to compensate for it.

What's the best way to count stitches? I get a different number of stitches every time.
You are not alone, especially when there are many stitches to count. Some of us can count for days, never coming up with the same number twice. Our solution is to use many, many stitch markers to divide the total number of stitches into small sections that are easy to count.

We use locking stitch markers so we can put them on the needle and take them off any time we want instead of having to wait until we knit the next row. You also can use leftover yarn that is about the same weight in a contrasting color by simply tying together the two ends of a 4-in. piece of yarn around the needle. The loop should be a little larger than the diameter of the needle so that it slips easily from needle to needle, but not so long that you knit it into your work. Cut off this marker when you don't need it anymore.

HOW TO READ A LACE PATTERN

Sometimes lace pattern instructions are written out in text using knitting abbreviations and sometimes they appear in charted form. Kind designers include both so you can use whichever is easier for you. Even kinder designers give you information on how many stitches/rows are in one repeat and how many, if any, stitches are needed to complete the pattern. We'll teach you how to read a lace pattern using written instructions. Once you understand this method, you can relate it to the charts you see. When you want to knit lace using charts and need a refresher in chart reading, see "How do I read a chart?" on p. 43.

The secret to trouble-free lace knitting

To knit lace without pulling your hair out, you must set up the first pattern row with stitch markers before you start to knit. Ignore this advice at your peril, and don't come running to us to help you straighten out your knitting.

Always place the stitch markers to match the asterisks in the text pattern. If the text changes the position of the asterisk, the instructions are telling you that the repeat will now begin in a different place, so you should change the stitch markers to match. We know that changing all the markers on the needle is boring, but if you don't, we can guarantee that you'll have troubles later on. As you become more proficient in lace knitting and learn to memorize patterns, there will come a time when you can do without stitch markers. If you need a refresher in understanding repeats, see "How many times do I have to repeat these instructions?" on p. 42.

Let's learn by knitting the Cat's Paw pattern from our Lace Sampler Wrap (see full pattern on p. 146). Using light-colored lightweight worsted yarn and size 9 needles (U.S.), cast on 56 sts. You may want to use the Double Start Cast On (see p. 123). It's very flexible, which is important when you are knitting lace because most lace has an open pattern and you don't want your cast on to create an unintentional pucker.

When you turn the work around to start the next row, you'll be facing the private side, so purl back and turn again. You're ready to set up the all-important first row.

Using your markers, mark off the two border stitches at each end of the needle. Count to make sure that there are 52 sts between the border markers. So far, so good.

Next, set up the pattern repeats at each asterisk using stitch markers of a different color (if you have them).

Row 1

K2, *k3, skp, yo, k1, yo, k2tog, k2, repeat from * one more time, k12, repeat from * 2 times, k2.

In other words: Your first marker is already in place after the 2 border sts. Place another marker after 10 sts (the first repeat). Place another marker after working 10 sts because the instructions tell you to repeat one more time, count off 12 sts and place another marker, count off 10 more sts and place marker, count off another 10 sts for the second repeat. You should now be at the other border marker.

Now that the markers are placed, knit the first row. If you don't understand an abbreviation in the instructions, there's a list of them at the back of the book, p. 153.

Continue to knit the next 7 rows of the Cat's Paw pattern, following the instructions. Because the pattern never changes the position of the asterisks (the repeats), you never have to change the position of the markers.

Repeat these 8 rows until you're comfortable with the lace pattern. End the last repeat after Row 6 to make the beginning rows and the end rows similar, and bind off *loosely*.

Congratulations! You are well on your way to understanding how to interpret the language of lace patterns.

My cast-on and bind-off stitches are too tight! What's the secret?
A flexible cast on and bind off are essential to lace, and we each use different methods to best achieve smooth transitions on and off the needle. Marion puts the tip of her right index finger on the needle after she casts on each stitch to make sure that the stitches are spread out across the needle with space between them. Ahza uses a larger size needle for the cast on so the cast-on row is not tighter than the rest of the work. Sometimes she casts on over both needles, and then removes one needle to continue.

If your bind off is too tight, and the finished piece draws together on the bind-off row, un-knit to where the problem begins and bind off *even more loosely*. If you just can't get it loose enough, try binding off with a larger needle.

There's a yarn over right before/right after my marker. When I work the next row, is the yarn over the last stitch of one repeat or the first stitch of the next one?
On the next row or round, count the number of stitches in between the last marker and the yarn over and check the instructions so you can replace the stitch marker in the correct place. If the yarn over keeps confusing you (and no wonder) you can make up your own repeats and shift the markers, making sure that they are not near any yarn overs.

The pattern for my triangular shawl says to integrate the extra stitches formed by the yarn overs by adding another pattern repeat. What does this mean?
Use a marker to separate the extra stitches from the beginning of what is now the first repeat. If you don't mind having little triangles at the sides of the shawl, knit or purl these extra stitches until you have enough of them to make a complete repeat and begin the extra repeat on the next public side row. If you do

The Double Start Cast On

This variation on the long-tail cast on is perfect for lace because of its flexibility. It adds stitches to the needle in pairs.

1. Put a slip knot on your needle and make the first cast-on stitch using the long-tail cast on (see p. 26).
2. Position your hands for another long-tail cast on stitch, and then readjust the yarn that goes over your thumb so that it goes directly from your palm (where you're holding both strands of yarn) around the back of your thumb, and then secure it as usual with your fingers.
3. Bring the point of the needle toward your palm and place it under the strand of yarn that goes behind your thumb and across your palm.
4. With the strand on your needle, swing your needle to your right and over the first strand on your index finger by moving the needle around the strand clockwise.
5. Bring the needle up through the loop of yarn around your thumb, slide your thumb out, and pull the yarn gently to tighten the stitch.
6. Put the yarn around your thumb in position for the long-tail cast on. You should have 3 sts on the needle, the slip knot and the pair of stitches that is the result of the long-tail cast on and the stitch that you just made.

Add additional pairs of cast-on stitches in the same way. If you need to cast on an even number of stitches, omit the last stitch of the final pair, ending with a long-tail cast-on stitch.

mind, then add on one stitch in pattern on each end until you've added a full repeat on each side. Place two new markers and start the process again. Of course, you will repeat this solution at the end of the row as well.

I keep knitting the wrong row of my chart. Am I going blind?

While we cannot offer medical advice in this book, we can offer advice on keeping all those chart rows straight. Some knitters make a copy of the chart and then draw a line through each row as they finish it. Some buy a magnetic board that comes with long, thin magnets. They place the chart on the board and highlight the row they are working with the magnets. We have recently discovered a marvelous new product, perhaps available at your local yarn store or office supply store, called transparent highlighter tape. This reusable tape comes in different colors and widths and works just like a highlighter marker—but it's easy to apply and remove. Place a strip of tape over the row that you are knitting, then peel it off and apply to each successive row as you work your way up the chart.

I forgot to do some of my yarn overs in the last row.
This mistake is easy to fix. Just lift the piece of yarn that is between the two stitches that surround the place where you forgot the yarn over and put it on your needle. Instant yarn over! Since lace is open by its nature, no one need ever know.

What do I do when I forget to make a decrease?
You can fix a missed decrease on the next row by taking out the 2 or 3 sts that you should have decreased, and make the decrease. This means you'll have some extra yarn at this spot, but you can loosen the stitches around it until the extra yarn disappears into the rest of the knitting. Again, no one need ever know.

I think that I screwed up the pattern about 20 rows back. Do I have to take the whole thing out and start over?
Not if you have unwaxed dental floss. If you don't have any in your Tool Kit (or your medicine cabinet), go out and buy some now. Unwaxed dental floss is the lifeline of lace knitters that prevents us from having to rip everything out and start again from the beginning.

PLACING A LIFELINE

To begin, identify a row of knitting that is correct and was fairly uncomplicated. A rest row—one without yarn overs or decreases—is perfect for this. Most of the time it will be the row below the row where you made the mistake. If the rest row is in garter stitch, look

Stitch Marker Tips

If you're casting on many, many stitches and are getting bored with counting the same stitches over and over again, read on for our time-saving tips:

- Place a stitch marker after every 50 (or whatever number you choose) sts. Continue placing stitch markers and recounting. It's much easier to count 50 sts twice than counting 400 sts again and again. Remove the stitch markers after you've achieved the correct number of cast-on stitches.
- When repeats have repeats inside of them, use more markers! Preferably in different colors coded to each type of repeat.
- There are some lace patterns, few and far between, thank goodness, that don't have the same number of stitches in each row. This means that you have to figure out how to best mark off sections. (We know you don't want to count those 400 sts after each row or round.) These are not patterns for the beginning lace knitter. Marion avoids them altogether, rationalizing that there are "so many stitch patterns, so little time."

Stitch Count Checklist

If you're knitting lace—or any other type of knitting using repeats—you'll be placing stitch markers on the first row. If you have too many stitches or too few after you finish placing your Row 1 markers, refer to the checklist below.

1. Recount the stitches to make sure your previous count was correct.

2. If you haven't placed stitch markers on the first row as suggested in this chapter, go get them and place them on the needle according to the instructions or chart. Chances are that you will identify the mistake at this point.

3. If you have stitch markers on the needle, check each section using the instructions and identify the section with the mistake.

4. Unknit back to the section and fix it. Then, check all the sections again.

5. Finish the row and count the stitches again. You should have the correct number of stitches.

6. If the number is still incorrect, you may have started with the wrong number of stitches. You'll have to unknit the whole row and check that you began with the correct number of stitches. But before you do this, put your knitting down and have a drink.

between the bumps for the Vs. It's not helpful to pick up the bumps, as the stitches will not appear on your needle correctly. Cut off a piece of the floss about 12 in. longer than the width of the piece where you made the mistake and thread it onto a tapestry needle.

Leaving a 6-in. tail (naturally), pick up the right-hand side of each of the stitches in this row. This is your lifeline. Take out your knitting until you reach the row that has been threaded with the dental floss. All the stitches should now be hanging from the floss.

Carefully transfer these stitches back onto your needle, checking the stitch mount as you go. If the lifeline is below the mistake and

the stitches are correct, knit on from the next pattern row. You need to replace the markers and count the stitches before you continue.

Some knitters who are just beginning to knit lace like to put in lifelines periodically, and we suggest that even more experienced knitters do so when knitting a complicated pattern or one with no rest rows. To add a lifeline as you go, put the dental floss in the row right underneath your needle. If you're knitting a pattern without rest rows, make sure that you catch any decreases and increases.

We bet that you can think of many other places to use lifelines as well.

It's going to take me many years to finish this project.

Probably not. Lace knitting gets easier and easier as you go along. You begin to memorize the patterns in a row and then memorize groups of rows. And then you'll come to the point where you can actually look at your knitting and see if you've made a mistake. For instance, if you have a strong vertical line of yarn overs and suddenly one is out of place, you know that something is not right.

I spent months on this shawl and it looks like a dishrag. And it's not even close to the pattern's finished measurements. What have I done wrong?

You haven't done anything wrong. That's exactly what lace knitting looks like before blocking. Lace needs to be blocked to open the holes and increase your project to its intended width. The surest way to block is to wash and rinse the piece, or soak it in tepid water before you block it. For our general treatise on blocking, see p. 99.

BLOCKING LACE

If the lace is very fine, you can try pinning it out first and using a spray bottle to wet it, adjusting the pins as needed. With thicker yarns you'll need to soak the project. You can also use the spray bottle to wet parts of the lace that have dried a little.

Gather your blocking tools: a spray bottle, blocking pins, and wires. If you don't want to invest in blocking wires, you'll need either a yardstick or a metal tape measure.

Lay the piece on towels or a blocking board. The surface should be slightly larger than the measurements given in the instructions. Pin down the two bottom corners of the work to the finished width measurement given in the pattern. Check the width and the straightness of the bottom line with the measuring tape or ruler. Put a book on one corner (to make sure

the corner is square), measure the length of the piece and pin each top corner.

Check your measurements, making sure that all the corners are square, and pin each side at the halfway points. Continue measuring, dividing in half, and pinning, until the pins are about 2 in. apart, or close enough that the sides are even.

When finished, let the piece dry completely, a minimum of 24 hours. When you take the pins out, the lace piece will be sized to the finished measurements and, best of all, will no longer look like a dishrag.

Some knitters block all their swatches even if the instructions don't ask for a blocked gauge. We feel that this is excessive (although technically correct), so we prefer to make lace projects that don't need to be knit to exact gauge. Please don't turn us in to the knitting police.

Knitting in 3-D, or Achieving Cable Competency

Why do cables elicit so much anxiety in many knitters, even experienced ones? The stitches, after all, are traditionally simple—stockinette stitches for the cable and a contrasting stitch such as reverse stockinette for the background.

We—okay, just Marion—used to be one of those fearful cable knitters. (It seems that Ahza can't remember a time when she didn't cable. She was a knitting child prodigy.) We think this fear of cabling has developed because every knitter has been taught that dropping stitches is an immediate crisis, and when working cables you deliberately drop stitches off your needles. Egad! Fortunately, the principles of cable knitting are easy to understand. Notice that we only said "understand." Executing cables requires practice and concentration, especially in the beginning.

Do Not Attempt This Lace Knitting at Home (Yet)

Knitting lace opens up an array of new yarn options, each more alluring and delicate than the next. Lace weight yarn, for example, is thinner than fingering or sock yarn. And then there is cobweb lace yarn, which is so fine that you can barely see it. In Marion's opinion, its sole purpose in knitting is to drive you crazy. This yarn is so light that you can hardly feel it on your needles, it seems to float, and it catches on everything, including fingernails and patches of rough skin. When it tangles, cobweb lace yarn immediately twists itself into a knot that is difficult, if not impossible, to undo. (Marion thinks that cobweb lace yarn does not want to be knit. Ahza thinks that Marion has some very strange ideas.) In any case, it's not the fiber for those just starting to explore lace knitting. The Lace Sampler Wrap pattern that we've written for you uses light worsted yarn on size 9 needles (U.S.), because lace knitting is easier to learn if you can see what you are knitting.

In addition to choosing the right weight yarn for your project and skill level, the color yarn you choose can impact a beginning lace knitter's success. We know that you want to knit that black lace mantilla. But restrain yourself for a bit. It's difficult to knit with black yarn when learning something new. Also, make sure that the color of your knitting needles contrasts with the color of the yarn that you are using. You'll never be able to see what you're doing if you try to knit a beige shawl on bamboo needles.

Cables are made by knitting one or more stitches out of order, and the process is called "turning the cable." It gives the appearance that stitches cross over each other on top of the knitted fabric. Special needles made just for cable work hold the reserved stitches. They can look like a double-pointed needle with a dip in the center, or have a hook at one end to secure the stitches. Some look like very short double-pointed needles. You can use a regular double-pointed needle, but it must be at least one size smaller than the needles with which you are knitting.

Although there seem to be more types of cables than you can shake a needle at, they differ in only three ways: the number of stitches in each cable, the direction in which the stitches are turned, and the number of rows between turning each cable—which can vary wildly in the same piece of knitting and even within an individual cable.

The number of stitches turned to make a cable can vary from as few as 1 st to as many as you can handle. In traditional knitting, the maximum number of turned stitches is usually 6 per side, for a total cable width of 12 sts.

To turn a cable, slide a certain number of stitches onto a cable needle, bring the cable needle either forward (in front of the public side), or back (on the private side). Work the next stitch or stitches from the left needle as instructed by your pattern, then work the stitches from the cable needle and continue.

We don't recommend that you eyeball the number of rows between turns, so we suggest that you keep track of the rows by using a row counter or a piece of paper and a pencil. Also, if you are turning a wide cable (and how wide depends on your pattern), you may develop a hole at the point where the cable turns. If you remember to pull the stitch after the turn tightly, the hole disappears.

Whether you bring the cable needle to the public or private side of the work affects the direction of the turn, and your pattern information will tell you whether to turn the cable to the right or the left. Designers write their instructions in a variety of ways, such as "cable 3 left," "C3L," or "cable 3/3 left." (Just swap in "right" or "R" and you're looking at instructions for a right-facing cable). Regardless of direction, just remember this: If you want the cable to twist to the left, bring the cable needle to the public side; if you want the cable to twist to the right, push the cable needle to the private side (Figures 4 and 5).

But it really works my nerves to have all those stitches hanging out, even if they are on a cable needle.

There *is* another way that might make you feel more secure: turning the cable before knitting any of the stitches. Begin by slipping the first stitches onto the cable needle, and then transfer the stitches that make up the other part of the cable from the left needle to the right needle. Transfer the stitches on the cable needle back to the left needle, and then the stitches that you just put on the right needle back onto the left one. Your cable has now been

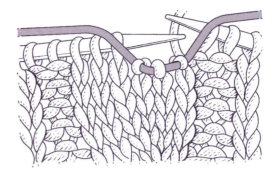

FIGURE 4
If you want a left-twisting cable, bring the stitches on the cable needle to the front of the work. This figure shows a cable 3 left, which is sometimes abbreviated as C3L or "cable 3/3 left."

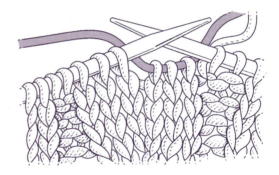

FIGURE 5
If you want a right-twisting cable, move the stitches on the cable needle to the back of the work. This figure shows a cable 3 right, which is sometimes abbreviated as C3R or "cable 3/3 right."

turned. Finish by knitting across all the stitches involved.

PRACTICE CABLING

We created a large cable surrounded by two sets of twisted stitches around the brim of the Updated Beanie with Cable on p. 135 to show you exactly how cables work. These cables are simple, but you will find more complicated cables in any stitch dictionary. The set of twisted stitches on each side of the cable looks like a 2-st cable, but it is worked without having to use a cable needle—bonus! The twist maneuver is safer because your stitches never leave the protection of the left needle. The Note section in our pattern instructions (see p. 136) explains how to make this right twist.

Remember that cable knitting is very impressive to non-knitters, and even to some knitters as well. You do want to impress others with your knitting prowess, don't you?

For practice, we're going to work the first repeat (28 rows) of the Updated Beanie with Cable. Even if you don't want to make the beanie you'll learn a lot about cables and learn to do a right twist.

To knit the sample, you either can use a fairly tightly spun yarn from your stash and the appropriately sized needles, or use our chosen yarn and needles. Find your cable needle or an equivalent (see p. 58).

Cast on 26 sts and work Rows 1 and 2 from the pattern instructions on p. 136.

On Row 3 you'll see a new abbreviation, RT, meaning *right twist*. (You'll find instructions for doing the right twist in the pattern.)

Now that you've done the twist, continue with pattern Rows 4–10. We've arrived at the turning row of the cable. It's Row 11 on the pattern, and when you've finished it you will have turned your first cable. Hooray! It wasn't that hard, was it? Now work Row 12, and then continue repeating Rows 13–28 to make as many cable repeats as you like, or follow the pattern as written to make the hat.

Note that an easy way to keep track of when to turn the cable is to look at the right twists. On every fourth twist, turn the cable.

What if my pattern says to cable but the instructions are different from yours?

All of us know that almost everything to do with knitting can be said in many different ways, so we're sure you're not surprised. If you're reading a chart, look at the key for stitches first, then the key for the cable. You can see in which direction the cable is turning by the slanted line and, by counting the boxes, how many total stitches in the cable.

Written instructions can be more difficult. Sometimes the number of stitches in a cable refers to the number of stitches counted over all of the stitches, and sometimes the number of stitches on each side before the turn. A good pattern writer should have left you a clue, so don't give up!

Why have spaces appeared on each side of my knitted cables?

Sometimes a cable will stretch away from the rest of the fabric. Try working the stitch before and after each cable through the back loops. When you twist a stitch, the stitch under it tightens and makes the hole in the row below disappear. This technique is also helpful if the cable has a hole between the two sets of stitches.

Why are my cables crooked?

If you knit the stitches in the cables too tightly, the stitches will draw in and distort the width of the row and cause crooked cables. The solution is to practice cabling until your hands adjust the tension of the individual cable stitches by instinct and your cables stand up smartly from the stitches around them. Knitting lots of cables is the only solution that we have found to be foolproof.

I finished what I thought was going to be my summer sweater but it's much too hot to wear. What kind of yarn should I use for cables?

Congratulations! It's your new winter sweater now. It doesn't matter that you used a lightweight yarn; most cables create an extra thickness in your knitting. When you begin to use cables, we advise using tightly twisted yarn, no lighter than sport weight. The twist in

The Left Twist

Even though you won't need to make a left twist in the Updated Beanie with Cable pattern, we're including instructions for it here to satisfy our need for symmetry. As with the right twist, the left twist is a look-alike to the 2-st cable but turns to the left. It's a shortcut, so if you're a real purist, you can use the traditional cable method. We're pretty pure, but not that pure.

To create a left twist: First knit the second stitch on the left needle through the back loop. With the right needle draw the loop behind the first stitch toward you but don't take the second stitch off the left needle. (You couldn't remove this stitch even if you wanted to, because it's boxed in by the adjacent stitches.) Keeping the loop on the right needle, knit the first stitch on the left needle and then drop both stitches off the left needle.

the yarn allows the cables to stand out from the background stitches. Cables in mohair, for example, would be one big mass of fuzz.

Why does the front of my cable sweater ripple?

Your tension when cabling will be tighter than when you are knitting flat. Look at the gauge instructions that came with your pattern. Some designers give two gauges: one for flat knitting and one for cable knitting. Make sure that both are correct. If you are still having a problem, try knitting the cable sections in a larger needle size. Or, you can do nothing and hopefully start a new fashion trend.

Where am I in the pattern?

Always keep track of row numbers and repeats because different cables may turn on different rows. You can buy a row counter or use pencil and paper. If your pattern is chartless you may want to write out each row on a separate index card, turning the cards over as you finish the row. If you are working from a chart you can highlight the row you're working on by using transparent highlighter tape.

I crossed my cable on the wrong row. Can I correct it?

You've got two options: Either rip back and reknit or just leave it alone (ask yourself, will anyone but me notice this?). But from here on out, always make sure that you keep track of the count between cable crosses. As we've already mentioned, eyeballing the rows can be deceptive.

I crossed my cable in the wrong direction. What should I do?

If you can't bring yourself to leave it as is, you'll have to rip back to the mistake and reknit. Or, you can follow our favorite solution and deliberately cross another cable or two in the same (wrong) direction to create a new design.

Why are the bind-off stitches on my cables flaring?

The stitches of a cable flare because they flatten out after the turn. To fix the flare, try knitting together the two center stitches of each part of the cable as you bind off. Bonus: You can also use this trick on any bind-off row if you're plagued by flaring stitches.

How can I get the private side of my cable scarf to look good?

The private side of a cabled fabric is generally not good enough to face the public. Keep it private. Of course, there is an exception to this. Lily Chin, who we think was the first, has created reversible cables to be used on projects, such as scarves, meant to be seen from both sides.

Is that all there is?

Not exactly. Sometimes many cables come out of one large cable, turn on their own and then come back into the large cable. Sometimes cables are uneven: The abbreviation "2/4 CR," for example, represents a cable with 2 sts passing over 4. You'll discover diagonal cables that sweep over the width of a sweater, cables that cross other cables, even small cables bursting forth from the top of a large one. We're sure you get the idea. Since you've mastered the basics, you'll be fine no matter what the chart or written instructions throw at you. Cable away.

Cabling without a Cable Needle

We would be remiss if we didn't tell you that there is *yet another* way of turning a cable—without using a cable needle at all. Once you become proficient at this technique, your cable knitting will go much faster because you don't need to keep slipping stitches on and off the cable needle. However, you may find it frightening at first.

When you're ready to turn the cable, free the stitches from the left needle and use the appropriate forefinger to hold them against the work below the needle to prevent them from unraveling. When you are ready to knit these stitches, slide them back onto the left needle. We don't recommend using this technique for a cable that is more than 6 sts wide because we can't hold more than 3 sts at one time with our index finger. However, this is our problem and there may be knitters who have bigger index fingers.

You have to practice this technique a lot before those stitches stop slipping out of your grasp and unraveling. It's for this reason that many knitters would rather sacrifice speed for certainty. We only use this method if we can't find anything to use as a cable needle and we're desperate to knit.

6

Apply Yourself: Six Patterns Looking for a Knitter

These six patterns will give you a chance to apply the skills that we've covered in Chapter 5—color work, lace, and cables. For those of you reading this book for the first time, we'd like to reassure you that you, too, can knit these patterns. Some, such as the Mosaic Mitts, take very little time, and others, such as the Lace Sampler Wrap, require more commitment. We've included patterns for every skill level, and there's even one pattern that you can knit with a friend. If we do say so ourselves, we like them and have our own versions that we use. Feel free to create your own versions as well.

Mosaic Mitts

This simple color knitting project is great for gift giving. Once you learn the chart pattern, you can knit a pair in an afternoon. Dive into your stash for unique color combinations, or choose a recipient's favorite colors. Best of all, two balls of yarn make three mitts, so knitting mitts for two friends means you get to keep a pair for yourself, too!

SKILL LEVEL
Intermediate

FINISHED MEASUREMENTS
- 7½-in. circumference
- 4½ in. high (women's size Medium)

YARN
- LB Collection® Cashmere by Lion Brand Yarn; 100% cashmere; 82 yd./75 m per ball; 1 ball each of Cruise #106 and Sprout #173. DK weight yarn

NEEDLE
- Size 6 U.S. (4 mm) needles, or size to obtain correct gauge

NOTIONS
- Tapestry needle

GAUGE
- 22 st to 4 in. over stockinette st.

NOTE
- These mitts are worked using the mosaic knitting technique. For detailed instructions and information on chart reading, see pp. 107–108.

MITTS (MAKE 2)

Mosaic Pattern

With the lighter color yarn, cast on 39 sts. Knit 3 rows.
Follow the Mosaic Mitts Chart Rows 1–18, remembering that, in mosaic knitting, every chart row equals 2 knitted rows.
With the lighter color, knit 4 rows. Decrease 1 st on the last row (38 sts).

Top Ribbing

Change to the darker color yarn.
With the public side facing, pick up and knit 38 sts.
Row 1 (private side)
P2, k2 across row, ending with p2.
Row 2 (public side)
K2, p2 across row, ending with k2.
Repeat Rows 1 and 2 until the Top Ribbing measures 1½ in., or desired length.
Work in k2, p2 rib for 1 in. or desired length, and bind off in pattern.

Wrist Cuff

With the public side facing, pick up and knit 38 sts with the darker color.

Row 1 (private side)
P2, k2 across row, ending with p2.
Row 2 (public side)
K2, p2 across row, ending with k2.
Repeat Rows 1 and 2 until the Wrist Cuff measures 1½ in., or desired cuff length.
Bind off in pattern.

FINISHING

Using the tapestry needle, sew up the side seam with a side-to-side join (see pp. 85–86), leaving a slot for the thumb. *Wear with pride!*

Tip: When making the second mitt, consider reversing the colors by knitting the dark chart squares and ribbing with the lighter color yarn and the blank chart squares with the darker color. You'll have enough yarn to make a third mitt, for those special friends who always lose one glove.

Mosaic Mitts Chart

Repeat

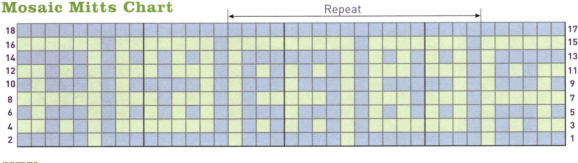

KEY

■ Darker color, Cruise
■ Lighter color, Spruce

Updated Beanie with Cable

Do you have Cable Phobia? Try our updated beanie with a twist or two. This pattern features a large cable bordered by small twists, so you're getting two techniques in one easy introduction to cabling. We think this project will cure you of any cable anxiety as you learn that cabling is all about knitting stitches out of order.

SKILL LEVEL
Intermediate

FINISHED MEASUREMENTS
- 21½-in. circumference
- 7 in. high (adult size Medium)

YARN
- Lion Brand Yarn Superwash Merino Cashmere; 72% superwash merino wool, 15% nylon, 13% cashmere; 87 yd./80 m per ball; 2 balls of #107 Sky. Worsted weight yarn (4)

NEEDLES
- Size 7 U.S. (4.5 mm) needles
- Size 9 U.S. (5.5 mm) circular needle, 16 in.,or 2 of any convenient length, or size to obtain correct gauge
- Size 9 U.S. (5.5 mm) double-pointed needles, if using one 16-in. circular needle
- Cable needle

NOTIONS
- 6 stitch markers
- Tapestry needle

GAUGE
- 4½ sts to 1 in. over stockinette st.

NOTE
- Here's how to do the Right Twist (RT)—the knitting version, not the dance step: Put the tip of your right needle into the front of the *second* stitch on your left needle and pull a loop of yarn through as usual, but leave the stitch on the left needle. Then, knit the *first* stitch on your left needle and pull both stitches off the left needle. You have knitted two stitches out of order, thus creating the Right Twist.

CABLE BAND
With the smaller needles, cast on 26 sts., using the long-tail cast on and leaving about an 18-in. tail for sewing. You will be working back and forth in rows.

Rows 1, 5 & 9 (RS)
K2, p2, k2, p2, k10, p2, k2, p2, k2.
Row 2 and all even numbered rows (WS)
K4, p2, k2, p10, k2, p2, k4.
Rows 3 & 7 (RS)
K2, p2, RT, p2, k10, p2, RT, p2, k2.

Row 11
K2, p2, RT, p2, [(turn cable) sl 5 sts to the cable needle and place in back of knitting; knit next 5 sts, then k5 sts from cable needle, pulling the first stitch tightly to avoid a hole], p2, RT, p2, k2.
Rows 13, 17, 21 & 25
K2, p2, k2, p2, k10, p2, k2, p2, k2.
Rows 15, 19 & 23
K2, p2, RT, p2, k10, p2, RT, p2, k2.
Row 27
K2, p2, RT, p2, [(turn cable) sl 5 sts to the cable needle and place in back; knit next 5 sts, then k5 sts from cable needle, pulling tightly to avoid hole], p2, RT, p2, k2.
Repeat Rows 13–28 seven times more for a total of 128 rows.
Then repeat Rows 1–10 once. Remember to decrease 1 st in the center of this last cable. (See p. 131.)
Bind off. The Cable Band should measure approximately 3½ in. wide when stretched slightly, and 21½ in. long.

CROWN
With the larger needle(s) of your choice, pick up and knit 96 sts evenly on a long side of the Cable Band (see "What am I supposed to do when a pattern tells me to 'pick up and knit'"? on pp. 53–54).
Join for working in the round.

Knit around in stockinette st. (knit every round) for 1 in., placing markers every 16 sts.

Decrease Rounds

Rnd 1
*Knit to 2 sts before marker, k2tog, sm, repeat from * to end of round (90 sts remain).

Rnds 2 & 3
Knit.

Rnd 4
*Knit to 2 sts before marker, k2tog, sm, repeat from * to end of round (84 sts remain).

Rnds 5 & 6
Knit.

Rnd 7
*Knit to 2 sts before marker, k2tog, sm, repeat from * to end of round (78 sts remain).

Rnd 8
Knit.

Rnd 9
*Knit to 2 sts before marker, k2tog, sm, repeat from * to end of round (72 sts remain).

Rnd 10
Knit.

Rnd 11
*Knit to 2 sts before marker, k2tog, sm, repeat from * to end of round (66 sts remain).

Rnd 12
Knit.

Tip: An easy way to know when to turn the cable is to look at the right twists. On every fourth repeat of the right twists, turn the cable. Thus, you may not need to keep track of which row you're working. Just count the twists!

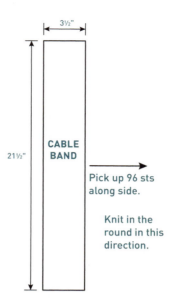

3½"

21½"

CABLE BAND

Pick up 96 sts along side.

Knit in the round in this direction.

Rnd 13
*Knit to 2 sts before marker, k2tog, sm, repeat from * to end of round (60 sts remain).

Rnd 14
Knit.

Rnds 15–22
*Knit to 2 sts before marker, k2tog, sm, repeat from * to ends of rounds until 12 sts remain.

Rnd 23
K2tog all around, removing markers (6 sts remain).

FINISHING

Cut yarn, leaving about an 8-in. tail.
Using the tapestry needle, thread the yarn tail through the remaining stitches. Pull together to close the opening.
Weave in the end on the wrong side.
Join together the ends of the cable band with the tail from your cast on (see "To join two pieces with bound-off edges end to end" on p. 90).
Weave in any remaining tails.
Block gently to widen the cable band and reveal your beautiful right twists.
Voila! You've mastered the cable technique while knitting an updated beanie.

Streamer Scarf

Marion made her first Streamer Scarf several years ago. After knitting the center, she knit all six streamers at the same time and on the same needle. It was yarn hell until she had the bright idea of knitting each streamer separately, and then knitting them together at center. Each succeeding scarf became wilder and wilder. Some were beautiful and some merely strange. Here, we've returned to that very first pattern to show you exactly how it's done.

SKILL LEVEL
Easy

FINISHED MEASUREMENTS
- One size fits all.

YARN
- LB Collection Angora Merino by Lion Brand Yarn; 80% extrafine merino, 20% angora; 131 yd./120 m per ball; 1 ball each of Sangria #196 (A), Blue Bonnet #108 (B), Blossom #103 (C), Avocado #174 (D), Nectarine #187 (E), and Pewter #152 (F) for back neck ribbing. DK weight yarn (3)

NEEDLES
- Size 8 U.S. (5.5 mm) needles, at least 9 in. long

NOTIONS
- Waste yarn or stitch holders
- Tapestry needle

GAUGE
Not important. You can make this scarf in any gauge and any weight yarn.

STREAMER SECTION 1
For all streamers, use the long-tail cast on.

Garter Stitch Streamer
Using yarn A, cast on 7 sts.
Every row
Sl1p, k6.
When the Garter Stitch Streamer measures 39½ in., put the stitches on a piece of waste yarn or stitch holder.

Seed Stitch Streamer
Using yarn B, cast on 7 sts.
Every row
*K1, p1, repeat from * to end of row.
When the Seed Stitch Streamer measures 39½ in., put the stitches on a piece of waste yarn or stitch holder.

Rib Stitch Streamer

Using yarn C, cast on 9 sts.

Row 1

K3, p3, k3.

Row 2

*K1, p1, repeat from * to end of row.

Repeat Rows 1 and 2 until Rib Stitch Streamer measures 39½ in. Put the stitches on a piece of waste yarn or stitch holder.

Moss Stitch

Using yarn D, cast on 8 sts.

Rows 1 & 2

*K2, p2, repeat from * to end of row.

Rows 3 & 4

*P2, k2, repeat from * to end of row.

Repeat Rows 1–4 until Moss Stitch Streamer measures 39½ in. Put the stitches on a piece of waste yarn or stitch holder.

Repeat the Seed Stitch Streamer instructions using yarn E to make the fifth Streamer.

Back Neck

Using yarn F, pick up and knit 30 sts across all streamers as shown. As you pick up the stitches, decrease each streamer to 6 sts using k2tog at each end of the streamer, and in the middle if you need to.

Work in k1, p1 rib until Back Neck measures 6 in. long.

STREAMER SECTION 2

On the public side, knit the first 6 Back Neck sts, increasing (we used kfb) to the number of sts for the Seed Stitch Streamer (7 sts). Put the remaining 24 Back Neck sts to be worked on a piece of waste yarn or stitch holder.

Follow the Seed Stitch Streamer pattern until the Streamer measures 39½ in. Bind off.

Knit across the next 6 Back Neck sts, increasing to the number of sts needed for the next streamer, worked in the stitch pattern and color

of your choice. Repeat for all remaining sts. For our Streamer Scarf, we reversed the order of colors and stitch patterns.

Weave in ends using the tapestry needle. You're finished! Place the scarf around your neck with the center ribbing behind your neck and arrange the streamers as you like.

Tip: This scarf can be a stash buster. Dig into it and choose different-colored balls of yarn that are the same weight. Yardage isn't that important because you can make more or fewer streamers of the same color. Of course you can always stripe the streamers.

Pillow of Many Colors

This pillow project lets you practice two kinds of color work at the same time. A traditional Fair Isle pattern is set into a simple intarsia background for the front of the pillow, while basic stripes liven up the back fabric. When knitting the front, you work some intarsia stitches, then work Fair Isle, then finish with more intarsia. Keeping track of each technique may present a challenge. Just remember that when knitting intarsia you leave your yarn behind, but with Fair Isle you bring it with you!

SKILL LEVEL
Experienced

FINISHED MEASUREMENTS
- 12 in. x 12 in.

YARN
- LB Collection 100% Superwash Merino by Lion Brand Yarn; 306 yd./280 m per ball; 1 ball each of Spring Leaf #174 (A), Peony #139 (B), Dijon #170 (C), Sky #107 (D), and Wild Berry #141 (E); DK weight yarn
  3

NEEDLES
- Size 6 U.S. (4 mm) needles, or size to obtain correct gauge

NOTIONS
- Pillow form to fit finished cover. (We used a 14-in. square form to make a firm, plump pillow.)
- Tapestry needle
- Highlighter tape (see p. 45)
- Hook-and-loop tape, optional

GAUGE
- 24 sts and 32 rows to 4 in. over stockinette st. Gauge is not *too* important here, as long as the pillow form doesn't show through your knitting.

CHART NOTE
- When reading the chart, read all odd numbered RS (knit) rows (public side) from right to left and all even-numbered WS (purl) rows (private side) from left to right. Use the Fair Isle technique, stranding colors on the private side for charted stitches, with the exception of the border stitches shown in color C. Use the intarsia technique to work the border stitches and the two outer sections not shown on the chart.

LOWER FRONT

Cast on 37 sts using yarn A and then 37 sts using yarn B for a total of 74 sts.

Row 1 (WS)

P37 sts in B, and then p37 sts in A, wrapping yarns at the color change according to the intarsia technique (see p. 113).

Row 2 (RS)

K37 sts in A, and then k37 sts in B, wrapping yarns at the color change as established. Repeat Rows 1 and 2 until work measures 4 in. from the cast-on edge, ending with Row 1.

FAIR ISLE

This 33-row section combines intarsia and Fair Isle techniques. See Chart Note.

Chart row 1

K15 sts with A. Follow the Pillow of Many Colors Chart for the next 44 sts. Knit remaining 15 sts with B.

Chart row 2

P15 sts with B. Follow the Pillow of Many Colors Chart for the next 44 sts. Purl remaining 15 sts with A.

Continue in stockinette st., following the chart for Rows 3–16, and working the outer stitches in A and B as established.

On Row 17 of the chart, knit the first 15 sts with E and last 15 sts with D. Follow the chart for the center 44 sts.

Continue with Chart rows 18–33.

UPPER FRONT

Hooray! From now on you only need to work with 2 colors, so you can put away all yarns but D and E.

K37 sts with E, and then k37 sts with D, wrapping yarns on the private side, following the intarsia technique.

On the next row, p37 sts with D, and then p37 sts with E, wrapping yarns as established.

Continue in stockinette st until piece measures 4 in. from the last chart row.

Bind off.

BACK (MAKE 2)

NOTE: The two Back pieces overlap at the center of the pillow, allowing you to insert the pillow form.

Using E, or the color of your choice, cast on 70 sts.

Knit 12 rows in garter st, approximately 1 in.

Working in stockinette st, knit the Back in a pat-tern of random stripes, varying the colors and widths to suit your fancy. Our stripes vary from 2 rows to 8 rows in width.

Continue until each Back piece measures at least 7 in., or more if you want a greater overlap. Bind off.

FINISHING

Weave in ends using the tapestry needle.

Block the two Back pieces separately to the same widths. Make sure that the two pieces will overlap in the center by at least 1 in.

Block the Front piece to the same width.

Join the Back pieces to the Front at the top and bottom. (See "To join two pieces with bound-off edges end to end" on p. 90.)

Join the sides, one back piece at a time and over-lapping them in the center, so they match the size of your front piece. (See "To join two pieces worked in stockinette side to side" on p. 87.)

Stuff your pillow form into your beautiful pillow cover and admire.

If there is a gap between the two back pieces (there was in ours), you can attach a strip of hook and loop tape to each side, as we did, to close.

Tip: To simplify this pattern, you could repeat just a portion of the chart, such as Rows 3–8. Or, you might choose to separate repeats with 2 rows of a contrasting color, or work each repeat in different colors. No boredom here! You will still be practicing Fair Isle and adding your own creativity to the pattern.

Pillow of Many Colors Schematic

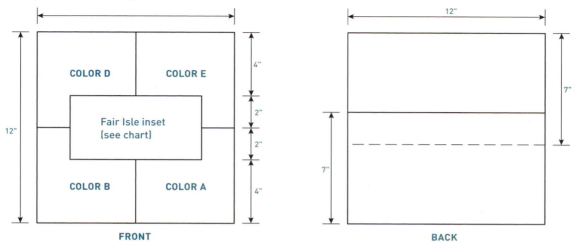

FRONT

BACK

Pillow of Many Colors Chart

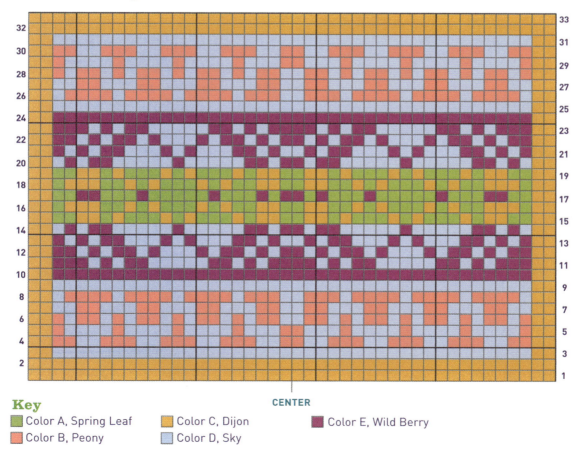

CENTER

Key

■ Color A, Spring Leaf   ■ Color C, Dijon   ■ Color E, Wild Berry

■ Color B, Peony   ■ Color D, Sky

Lace Sampler Wrap

This wrap features five different lace patterns to help you practice lace knitting and improve your ability to read lace charts. When we made the sample shown here, we each knit one side of the wrap, and then joined together our pieces for a truly collaborative project. To make this project with your own knitting buddy, read on. We'll tell you how.

FINISHED MEASUREMENTS
- 15 in. x 76 in., blocked

YARN
- LB Collection Cotton Bamboo by Lion Brand Yarn; 52% cotton, 48% rayon from bamboo; 245 yd./244 m per ball; 3 balls of #139 Hibiscus. DK weight yarn ⟨3⟩

NEEDLES
- Size 9 U.S. (5.5 mm) needles, or size to obtain an open lace fabric, usually 2–3 sizes larger than the size recommended on your yarn label

NOTIONS
- 10 stitch markers
- Tapestry needle

GAUGE
- Not important. When knitting with a friend, make sure your gauges match.

NOTE
- For each pattern, work the first pattern row as follows: K2, pm, work 52 sts in pattern, pm, k2. These outer stitches, 2 on each side, are the Edge Stitches, and are knit on every row throughout the entire project, creating garter st borders, so the patterns are written for the center 52 sts only.
  Continue knitting Edge Stitches throughout even when not indicated in the charts on pp. 148–149 or pattern instructions.

SIDE ONE
Cast on 56 sts, using the Double Start Cast On (see p. 123). You will be working back and forth in rows.
Knit back.

Eyelet Pattern

NOTE: Edge Stitches are included in Eyelet Pattern instructions.

Row 1 (RS)

K2, sm, *k2tog, yo, repeat from * to last 2 sts (marker), sm, k2.

Row 2 and all even numbered rows (WS)

K2, sm, purl to last 2 sts, sm, k2.

Row 3

K2, sm, *yo, k2tog, repeat from * to last 2 sts, sm, k2.

Row 4

Work as written for Row 2.

Repeat Rows 1–4 three times more for a total of 16 rows.

Knit 2 rows, slipping markers.

Cat's Paw Pattern

NOTE: Placing markers at asterisks will help you keep track of the repeats. Edge Stitches are not included in chart or pattern instructions.

Row 1

*K3, skp, yo, k1, yo, k2tog, k2. Repeat from * once more. K12. *K3, skp, yo, k1, yo, k2tog, k2. Repeat from * once more.

Rows 2, 4, 6 & 8

Purl.

Row 3

*K2, skp, yo, k3, yo, k2tog, k1. Repeat from * once more. K12. *K2 , skp, yo, k3, yo, k2tog, k1. Repeat from * once more.

Row 5

*K4, yo, sk2p, yo, k3. Repeat from * once more. K12. *K4, yo, sk2p, yo, k3. Repeat from * once more.

Row 7

Knit.

Repeat Rows 1–8 four times for a total of 32 rows.

Knit 2 rows.

Eyelet Pattern

Work Eyelet Pattern to separate Cat's Paw Pattern from the pattern that follows.

Knit 2 repeats, or 8 rows, of Eyelet Pattern. Knit 2 rows.

Checkered Acre Pattern

NOTE: Multiple of 10 sts, plus 2.

Row 1

K2, *yo, k2tog, k4, skp, yo, k2. Repeat from * to Edge Stitches.

Row 2

Purl.

Repeat Rows 1 and 2 four times for a total of 8 rows.

Row 9

K3, *skp, yo, k2, yo, k2tog, k4. Repeat from *, ending the last repeat k3 at marker.

Row 10

Purl.

Repeat Rows 9 and 10 four times for a total of 16 rows.

Repeat these 16 rows twice for a total of 32 rows.

Repeat Rows 1–8 once more for a total of 40 rows.

Knit 2 rows.

Eyelet Pattern

Work the Eyelet pattern to separate Checkered Acre Pattern from the pattern that follows.

Knit 2 repeats, or 8 rows, of Eyelet Pattern.

Knit 2 rows.

Miniature Leaf Pattern

NOTE: Multiple of 6 sts, plus 4.

Row 1

K2, *k2tog, yo, k1, yo, ssk, k1; repeat from * 8 times (48 sts), k2.

Rows 2, 4, 6 & 8

Purl.

Tip: The lovely, small Miniature Leaf pattern would make a handsome scarf all by itself.

Row 3
K1, k2tog, *yo, k3, yo, sl2 kwise, k1, p2sso (center double decrease, or cdd); rep from *, end last repeat ssk, k2.

Row 5
K2, *yo, ssk, k1, k2tog, yo, k1; rep from * 8 times (48 sts), k2.

Row 7
K2, *k1, yo, sl2 kwise, k1, p2sso (cdd), yo, k2; rep from *, end last repeat k2.
Repeat Rows 1–8 six times for a total of 48 rows.
Knit 2 rows.

Eyelet Pattern

Work the Eyelet pattern to separate Miniature Leaf Pattern from the pattern that follows.
Knit 2 repeats, or 8 rows of Eyelet Pattern.
Knit 4 rows. The extra rows will make it easier to graft the two sides of the wrap together.

Diamond and Gull's Wings Pattern

As a challenge, we're only providing the chart for this pattern—no written instructions included. Don't forget to include your Edge Stitches. You can do it!
Work the 40 rows of the Diamond and Gull's Wings Pattern Chart.
Knit 2 rows.

Tip: Make this project your own by choosing just a few of these patterns and repeating them more times until the wrap reaches your desired length. You also could choose to knit the patterns in a different order, or just pick one pattern for the entire wrap. Just remember to maintain your Edge Stitches to minimize curling along the edges.

Shetland Lace Lore

The Lace Sampler Wrap features an array of traditional patterns from the Shetland Islands. The handsome openwork lace in the Checkered Acre pattern, for example, is reminiscent of plowed fields, thus the name "Acre."

Most Shetland Islanders would knit lace to supplement their income, so speed and ease of knitting were of great importance. That's why many of the patterns are easy to memorize and alternate a lace row with a rest row. Shetland patterns were handed down from knitter to knitter, and some knitters would take a piece of "sampler" knitting with them wherever they went so that they always could record new combinations of stitches. Although Shetland patterns are simple in themselves, finished pieces were designed to look complicated (and more expensive) by combining patterns—just like our Lace Sampler Wrap.

SIDE TWO

If you are knitting this wrap by yourself, you can continue from this point, knitting all the patterns in reverse order. Always knit the 2 rows that separate the patterns. When you finish, bind off loosely.

If you are knitting with a friend, your partner should work a second piece identical to the first, from the beginning cast on through the last Eyelet Pattern, stopping before Diamond and Gull's Wings Pattern. Then, knit 2 rows. When we made the Sampler shown, Ahza knit Side One, including the Diamond and Gull's Wings Pattern, and Marion knit Side Two. Then, we used the Kitchener stitch (see pp. 93–94) to join the two pieces, following the method for grafting garter stitch.

We hope you have congratulated yourself (or selves) upon finishing this project. It is truly a great accomplishment!

Eyelet Pattern Chart

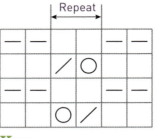

Key

☐ K (RS), P(WS)   ☑ K2tog
⊟ K (WS)   ☉ Yo

Miniature Leaf Pattern Chart

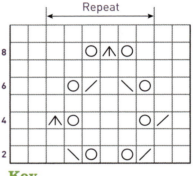

Key

☐ K (RS), P(WS)   ☑ K2tog   ☉ Yo
                    ◩ Ssk   ⋀ Sl2 kwise,
                                       k1, 2sso

Checkered Acre Pattern Chart

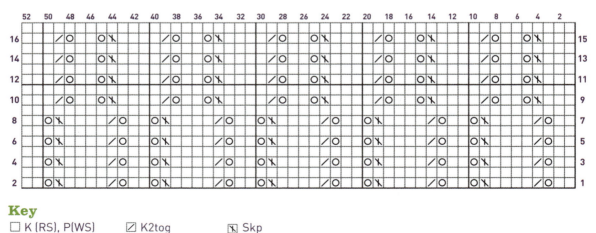

Key

☐ K (RS), P(WS)   ☑ K2tog   ◩ Skp
                                    ☉ Yo

Cat's Paw Pattern Chart

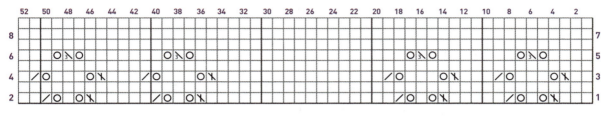

Key

☐ K (RS), P(WS)	◩ Sk2p	◪ Skp
◿ K2tog	☉ Yo	

Diamond and Gull's Wings Pattern Chart

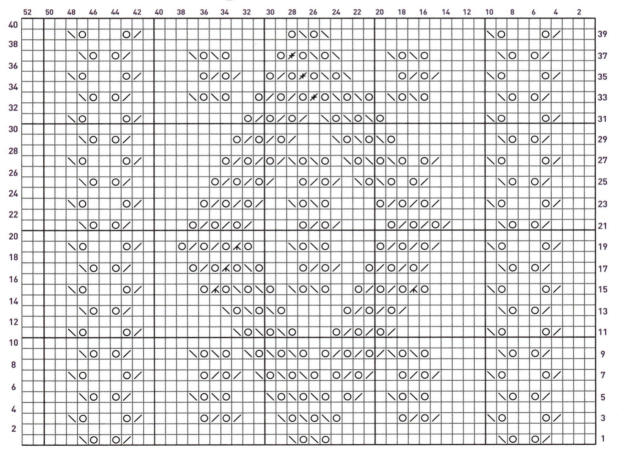

Key

☐ K (RS), P(WS)	◉ K3tog	◉ Sl2, k3tog, p2sso
◿ K2tog	◺ Ssk	☉ Yo

The Deliberate Drop Stitch Scarf

Here's your chance to make a "mistake" to your heart's content. In this pattern you can embrace your inner knitting rebel and love your dropped stitches! Just put them where you want them and watch a new pattern emerge. We call this "The Deliberate Drop."

SKILL LEVEL
Easy

FINISHED MEASUREMENTS
- 5 in. x 50 in.

YARN
- Rowan® Belle Organic DK; 50% organic cotton, 50% organic wool; 131 yd./120 m per ball; 2 balls Persimmon #004. DK weight **3**

NEEDLE
- Size 6 U.S. (4 mm) needles, or size to obtain correct gauge

NOTIONS
- 3 stitch markers
- Row counter or pencil and paper
- Tapestry needle
- Large crochet hook, for fringe

GAUGE
- 22 sts to 4 in. over stockinette st.

NOTES
- Slip the first stitch as if to purl on every row throughout the scarf. This will be indicated using the abbreviation *sl1p* on pattern rows.
- The Deliberate Drop Stitch: Drop the stitch off the needle and unravel down to the yarn over 6 rows below the working row, creating horizontal "ladders" in your scarf. You can unravel the drop stitches as you go, or wait till you are finished with your scarf and enjoy unraveling all at once!

SCARF

Cast on 32 sts loosely, using the long-tail cast on.

First row

Sl 1st st as if to purl, then k31.

Preparation row

Sl1p, k2, *pm, p2, k1, yo, k1, p2, k2. Repeat from * 2 times more; end p2, k3 (35 sts). (You will be working on 35 sts until "How to End.")

Rows 1, 3 & 5

Sl1p, k1, p1, *sm, k2, p2, k2, p3. Repeat from * 2 times more; end k2, p1, k2.

Rows 2 & 4

Sl1p, k2, *sm, p2, k3, p2, k2. Repeat from * 2 times more; end p2, k3.

Row 6

Sl1p, k2, *sm, p2, k1, drop next st using the Deliberate Drop Stitch (see Notes), k1, p2, k1, yo, k1. Repeat from * 2 times more; end p2, k3.

Rows 7, 9 & 11

Sl1p, k1, p1, *sm, k2, p3, k2, p2. Repeat from * 2 times more; end k2, p1, k2.

Rows 8 & 10

Sl1p, k2, *sm, p2, k2, p2, k3. Repeat from * 2 times more; end p2, k3.

Row 12

Sl1p, k2, *sm, p2, k1, yo, k1, p2, k1, drop next st using the Deliberate Drop Stitch, k1. Repeat from * 2 times more; end p2, k3.

Repeat Rows 1–12 until your scarf measures 50 in., or your desired length. Remember to save some yarn for fringe if you want some! Before beginning your last ball, cut 32 pieces of yarn each about 10 in. long for the fringe. This way you can knit until the ball is almost finished.

How to end

When you get to your very last Row 12, work in pattern, removing the markers and omitting the yarn overs. You will have restored your original stitch count of 32 sts.

Knit 1 row. Bind off.

FRINGE

Hold 2 of your fringe strands of yarn together and fold in half. Insert the large crochet hook through the edge of the scarf and pull the folded loop through. Then, draw the ends through the loop and tighten. Position 8 pairs of strands evenly at the beginning and end of the scarf. Wear with pride!

ABBREVIATIONS: A MAGIC DECODER

Abbreviation	Translation	Abbreviation	Translation
"	inch(es)	p2tog	purl 2 sts together
alt	alternate	p2togtbl	purl 2 sts together through the back loops (left-slanting decrease)
approx	approximately	prev	previous
beg	begin(ning)	psso	pass slipped stitch(es) over
bet	between	pwise	purlwise
BO	bind off	rem	remain(s)(ing)
CC	contrasting color	rep	repeat(s)
CO	cast on	rev St st	reverse stockinette stitch
cm	centimeter(s)	RH	right hand
cont	continu(e)(ing)	rnd(s)	round(s)
dec	decreas(e)(es)(ing)	RS	right side, public side, or right-hand side
dpn	double-pointed needle(s)	RT	right twist
foll	follow(s)(ing)	sk	skip
g	gram	skp	slip, knit, pass slip stitch over (left-slanting decrease)
in.	inch(es)	sk2p	slip1, knit 2 together, pass slip stitch over the knit 2 together (2-st decrease)
inc	increase(e)(es)(ing)		
k2tog	knit 2 sts together through the front loops (right-slanting decrease)		
		sl	slip
k2togtbl	knit 2 sts together through the back loops (left-slanting decrease)	sl1k	slip 1 knitwise
		sl1p	slip 1 purlwise
k or K	knit	sm	slip marker
kfb	knit into the front and back of the next stitch (increase)	ssk	slip 1 knitwise, slip 1 knitwise, place stitches back onto the left needle, knit these 2 sts together through back loops (left-slanting decrease)
kwise	knitwise		
LH	left hand, private side, or left-hand side.		
lp(s)	loop(s)	sl st	slip stitch(es)
LS	left side	st(s)	stitch(es)
LT	left twist	St st	stockinette stitch/stocking stitch
m	meter(s)	tbl	through back loop(s)
M1	make 1 st	tog	together
M1 p-st	make 1 purl st	WS	wrong side, private side
MC	main color	wyib	with yarn in back
mm	millimeter(s)	wyif	with yarn in front
oz.	ounce(s)	yd.	yard(s)
p or P	purl	yfwd	yarn forward
pat(s) or patt(s)	pattern(s)	yo	yarn over
pm	place marker		

Further Reading

Here's a list of some of our favorite knitting reference books to help you solve emergencies that we haven't covered (there are a few, we admit). You can use them to explore further some of the techniques we have written about.

Stanley, Montse. *Knitter's Handbook*. Pleasantville, NY. Reader's Digest, 1993. (Extremely comprehensive reference book. An oldie but goody.)

Wiseman, Nancie M. *The Knitter's Book of Finishing Techniques*. Woodinville, WA. Martingale & Company, 2002. (This is a good book for expanding your finishing skills.)

There are many stitch dictionaries, but we think Barbara Walker will keep you in stitches for years to come:

Walker, Barbara. *The Treasury Set: Volumes 1–4*. Stevens Point, WI. Schoolhouse Press, 1998. (This is a collection of her first four books. Every volume has a great variety of stitches.)

If you'd like to have more stitch patterns for mosaic knitting:

Walker, Barbara. *Mosaic Knitting*. Stevens Point, WI. Schoolhouse Press, 1997. (This edition contains stitch patterns not previously published in the original collection.)

Fair Isle sweaters have an interesting history and special construction techniques. If you'd like to learn absolutely everything you need to know to make these traditional sweaters:

Starmore, Alice. *Alice Starmore's Book of Fair Isle Knitting*. Mineola, NY, Dover Publications, 2009.

For more about lace knitting:

Swansen, Meg. *A Gathering of Lace*. Sioux Falls, SD. XRX Books, 2005. (A compilation of designs from many lace traditions and from many experts.)

Sweaters covered with cables are often called Aran knitting. For more on this type of knitting, refer to Starmore's book of the same name. The original is long out of print. Thank goodness that Dover has reprinted most of her older books.

Starmore, Alice, *Aran Knitting*. Mineola, NY. Dover Publications, 2010.

Before We Bind Off

In our view, knitting should always be rewarding to the knitter—sometimes fun, sometimes relaxing, sometimes meditative, but always enjoyable. We wrote this book for the times when knitting is confusing and/or exasperating to provide you with a shoulder to cry on and a source of tried-and-true advice. Whatever your knitting problem, know you're not alone and that making mistakes is part of the process.

Yours in Wool,
Ahza & Marion

Index

....